TAMIRIS
A Chronicle of Her Dance Career
1927-1955

"Tamiris," original drawing by Léopold Gottlieb, reproduced on a program for the Salle Rudolf Steiner, July 5 1928 Tamiris concert
Dance Collection

TAMIRIS
A Chronicle of Her Dance Career
1927-1955

BY CHRISTENA L. SCHLUNDT

New York
The New York Public Library
Astor, Lenox and Tilden Foundations
1972

Copyright © 1972 The New York Public Library
Library of Congress Catalog Card Number: 72-86181
International Standard Book Number: 0-87104-233-9

TABLE OF CONTENTS

	Introduction	7
1	Early Concert Years, 1927-1929	10
2	The Experimental Years, 1930-1933	14
3	Tamiris and Her Group, 1934-1936	27
4	Tamiris and Her Sense of Mission, 1936-1939	38
5	Tamiris' Studio Theatre, 1940-1944	61
6	Miss Tamiris on Broadway, 1944-1955	68

Illustrations
(FOLLOWING PAGE 32)

INTRODUCTION

ANY HISTORY of the dance in twentieth-century America which omits the career of Helen Becker, early known as Tamiris and then Helen Tamiris, forfeits a vivid chapter. Neither as dully serious nor as ascetically cerebral as her contemporaries, she was more modern than any in that essence of modernity: a responsiveness to the unformulated will of an epoch, a drive to do what a time required.

Tamiris was also modern in her use of movement as the substance of the art of dance. This is only an arty way of saying that Tamiris could really move. Tamiris in motion excited the most casual observer with her rich loveliness, her heroic and maenadic femaleness, her animal logic, her ease, flow, control, range. In vigorous affirmation of life, she seemed to wring her dances from her blood and muscle. European reviewers identified a lust for movement that was overwhelming. With this virtue of vital movement, the art of Tamiris was more ephemeral than most dancing, the most ephemeral of all arts. When Tamiris ceased to move, her art was gone because Tamiris movement was inextricably Tamiris art.

In tracing the career of such a transient being, one can only suggest the multiplicity of a career attuned to the moment. That moment happened to be that period of lacerating change in America, the middle third of the twentieth century. This account of her life concentrates on four of her reactions to this upheaval. The first part deals with her entrance on to the concert stage, the second with her formulation of the Dance Repertory Theatre idea, and, after its demise, her establishment of her "Group," the third with her efforts in Federal Theatre, and a fourth part with her contribution to musical comedy theatre. This account attempts to list all her major appearances as a dancer and her major presentations as a choreographer. It includes for each dance the title, the choreographer if known, the composer or arranger of the accompaniment, and the names of the performing dancers listed as they were spelled on the programs. Pertinent material about other dancers who appeared on the same programs with Tamiris is included in footnotes or in brackets. A glance through this chronicle reveals how many lives the mercurial Tamiris touched, how wide her influence was.

For the main purpose of this account is to suggest the scope of the activities of this vivid human being. In the first part of her career, she let loose the scream of a siren in the sacred grounds of the concert stage. There she showed her beautiful legs in order to express the power she derived from her base, the floor. There she put a flower in her shockingly red hair when other modern dancers were wearing hair shirts.

Once precariously established, she saw that others were financially as innocent as she. Her proposal to band dancers together administratively in the Dance Repertory Theatre was uneasily accepted for only two years. After that, each modern dancer went her own way, to continue not only the solitary drive to personal reputation but also the American dance tradition of fiscal irresponsibility. Failing to unify the major modern dancers in mundane matters, Tamiris turned to her pupils and to the problems of her— and their—time. She united both in group works with social themes.

In the American Dance Association formed in the middle and late thirties, Tamiris, as leader in its founding and president during its existence, tried again to organize dancers for their common benefit. Responding to another element of the thirties, she was one of those who convinced Hallie Flanagan, director of Federal Theatre, to recognize dance in the structure of the Works Progress Administration. Reacting amidst the confusion of other recalcitrant dancers, Tamiris alone built a continuity of respectable dance production in that arena of American aspirations.

Finally, following the senseless slaughter of Federal Theatre and the ensuing collapse of the American Dance Association, this woman, now calling herself Helen Tamiris, helped bring respect and excellence to another part of the world of dance, the musical comedy. There her collaboration with other artists satisfied for over a decade her need to work with and bring out the best in other human beings.

Permeating the life of the vital Tamiris was the drive toward cooperative action, based on her existential love of the moment full of flesh and blood people with here-and-now problems. Her awareness of the excitement of the living moment in all its manifestations, the sordid as well as the sublime, has had an immeasurable influence on keeping modern dance modern. But her solution of "creative collaboration," tried first in the Dance Repertory Theatre, next in the American Dance Association and the Federal Dance Theatre, and then in musical comedy, is a legacy still ignored by dancers.

The sources of this account are: the programs and clippings of Helen

Introduction 9

Tamiris, Louis Horst, and Hanya Holm, the issues of the *Dance Herald*, the files of Federal Dance Theatre and the American Dance Association, all in the Dance Collection of the Performing Arts Research Center of The New York Public Library at Lincoln Center; programs and reviews from the archives of the Theatre Collection of the same library; the pertinent issue of *The Dance Observer, Dance Magazine* (in all its manifestations), and the New York *Times*. Annotation for the few published works referred to can be found in the footnotes.

The support and cooperation of Miss Genevieve Oswald, Curator of the Dance Collection, and the members of her staff have been invaluable. This research was carried out with monetary support from Intramural Research Grant No 9067, the University of California, and with help in research from the University's Reference Department, especially Miss Dorothea M. Berry, Head.

Caricature of Tamiris, by Aline Fruhauf, from the *Dance Observer*, April 1934   *Dance Collection*

1 EARLY CONCERT YEARS, 1927–1929

HELEN BECKER HAD a varied preparation for her career as a dancer: children's dance at the Neighborhood Playhouse, Italian ballet at the Metropolitan Opera, Russian ballet at Michel Fokine's studio, natural dancing from a Duncan studio. She served performing apprenticeship as a member of the corps of the Metropolitan Opera Ballet, as a leading soloist in the Bracale Opera Company in a tour of South America, as a specialty dancer in night clubs and revues and in the stage shows of movie houses, and as a featured dancer in the 1924–25 Music Box Revue. Why she gave up remunerative work to move onto the penurious concert stage can only be answered by the reason given by all of the modern dancers assaulting the concert field during the last three years of the 1920s: they were dissatisfied with dance as it was and determined to reform it. Helen Becker took the name of a ruthless queen Tamiris and also entered the concert arena on October 9 1927, following Martha Graham by one year. As she, the new Tamiris, declared in a statement titled "Manifest" printed on her second concert program:

> Art is international, but the artist is a product of a nationality and his principal duty to himself is to express the spirit of his race. . . .
> There are no general rules. Each original work of art creates its own code.
> The aim of the dance is not to narrate (anecdotes, stories, fables, legends, etc), by means of mimic tricks and other established choreographical forms. Dancing is simply movement with a personal conception of rhythm.
> Costumes and music are complements of the dance. A dancer's creation should stand the test in the nude and the experience of motion without music. . . .

Thus she rejected the dance past with its mimed stories, its theatricality and atmosphere: she would follow no rules; she would react.

In twenty-seven solo dances created in two years, she made her physical statement in seven programs—four in New York and three in Europe. Immediately, she was the entity, Tamiris, the dancer: American modern, a reflection of all that was urban in *Dance of the City* with its siren accompaniment, a suggestion of all that was Hemingway in *Impressions of the Bull Ring* with its flashing colors, a foreshadowing of all that was to be concert jazz dance in *1927* with its Gershwin rhythms, a summary of all that meant "Champion of . . ." in *Prize Fight Studies* with its inimitable opening swagger, a glimpse of all that was Freudian in *Subconscious* with its unabashed nudity, a statement of all that was "sex" in *Twentieth Century Bacchante* with its frank voluptuousness. She attacked affected Madonna interpretations in *Hypocrisy*. In *The Queen Walks in the Garden*, she moved in silence. She forever encompassed the spirit of the Negro spiritual as her own métier

Early Concert Years, 1927-1929

by moving to the three songs *Nobody Knows de Trouble I See*, *Swing Low, Sweet Chariot*, and *Joshua Fit de Battle ob Jericho*. And she sounded the call of the next decade in *Revolutionary March* with three kettle drums resounding alone, a flag-like costume—here were the awakenings of the social Tamiris. In all her dances, the "Harlem savage," as she was also called, recognized life as conflict and said so verbally, physically, and artistically.

This first period revealed to the dance world the individual, Tamiris the dancer. It delineated her as a force, despite her childlike wonder, to be reckoned with in the new dance not even yet named. There is also evidence of the leader Tamiris, the choreographer of dances for others. In the fall of 1929, she announced her School of the American Dance to attract a nucleus for a "group."

That same fall, she showed her penchant for the world of musical comedy, as a choreographer in the Experimental Theatre's production of *Fiesta*, a play by Michael Gold, one of the editors of *The Masses*. Closely woven into the third act, her whirling exciting festival scene in a plaza added dimension to the otherwise unsuccessful play about pedestrian revolutionaries in Mexico.

First Concert Program

Oct 9 1927 eve   New York: Little Theatre   Presented by Daniel Mayer, Inc

Dance Moods

Florentine (Tamiris / Paladine) Tamiris; *Melancholia* (Tamiris / Debussy) Tamiris; *Portrait of a Lady* (Tamiris / Florent Schmitt) Tamiris; *Circus Sketches* (Tamiris / John Powell) Tamiris; *The Queen Walks in the Garden* (Tamiris / no music) Tamiris; *Three Kisses* (Tamiris / Berger) Tamiris; *Two Poems* (Tamiris / Scriabin) Tamiris; *Impressions of the Bull Ring* (Tamiris / R. Calleja) Tamiris; *Tropic* (Tamiris / Cyril Scott) Tamiris; *Amazon* (Tamiris / Louis Gruenberg) Tamiris; *Subconscious* (Tamiris / Debussy) Tamiris; *1927* (Tamiris / George Gershwin) Tamiris

Piano, Louis Horst; costumes, Tamiris; decoration for *1927*, Juan Oliver

Second Concert Program

Jan 29 1928 eve   New York: Little Theatre   Presented by New Art Circle

Dance Moods

Moods Diverse: *Gayety* (Tamiris / Florent Schmitt) Tamiris; *Perpetual Movement* (Tamiris / Poulenc) Tamiris; *Country Holiday* (Tamiris / Dent Mowry) Tamiris; *Hypocrisy* (Tamiris / Satie) Tamiris; *Portrait of a Lady* Tamiris; *Impressions of the Bull Ring* Tamiris

American Moods: *Harmony in Athletics* (Tamiris / Louis Gruenberg) Tamiris; *Two Spirituals: Nobody Knows de Trouble I See* (Tamiris / arr J. R. Johnson) and *Joshua Fit de Battle ob Jericho* (Tamiris / arr Lawrence Brown) Tamiris; *Circus Sketches* Tamiris; *Twentieth Century Bacchante* (Tamiris / Louis Gruenberg) Tamiris; *Prize Fight Studies* (Tamiris / beating of piano strings) Tamiris; *1927* Tamiris

Piano, Louis Horst; costumes, Tamiris; decorations, Juan Oliver

Paris Performance

5 Juillet 1928 eve   Paris: Salle Rudolf Steiner   Présentée par Jan Sliwinski

Gaîté [Gayety] Tamiris; *Hypocrisie [Hypocrisy]* Tamiris; *Rythmes Paysans [Peasant Rhythms—of worship, joy, toil]* (Tamiris / Stravinsky) Tamiris; *Impressions d'une Corrida [Impressions of the Bull Ring]* Tamiris; *Portrait d'une Dame [Portrait of a Lady]* Tamiris; *Harmonie d'Athlétisme [Harmony in Athletics]* Tamiris; *Sketches de Cirque [Circus Sketches]* Tamiris; *1927* Tamiris; *Bacchante du Vingtième Siècle [Twentieth Century Bacchante]* Tamiris; *Deux Spirituals Nègres [Nobody Knows de Trouble I See and Joshua Fit de Battle ob Jericho]* Tamiris; *Subconscient [Subconscious]* Tamiris; *Etudes de Boxe [Prize Fight Studies]* Tamiris

Piano, Daniel Lazarus; costumes, Tamiris

Salzburg Festival Performance

Aug 7 1928   Salzburg: Stadt Theatre   Presented by the Mozarteum Society

Gayety Tamiris; *Hypocrisy* Tamiris; *Perpetual Movement* Tamiris; *Peasant Rhythms* Tamiris; *Portrait of a Lady* Tamiris; *Impressions of the Bull Ring* Tamiris; *1927* Tamiris; *Harmony in Athletics* Tamiris; *Two Spirituals* Tamiris; *Circus Sketches* Tamiris; *Twentieth Century Bacchante* Tamiris; *Prize Fight Studies* Tamiris

Piano, Felix Petyrek; costumes, Tamiris

Berlin Performance

Feb 16 1929 midnight   Berlin: Gloria Palast   Presented by Novembergruppe

"Nacht Vorstellung"

American Serenade 1 (Sonatina for Radio) (Tamiris / George Antheil) Tamiris; *American Serenade 2 (Sonatina for Radio)* (Tamiris / George Antheil) Tamiris; *Two Spirituals* Tamiris; *Harmony in Athletics* Tamiris; *Prize Fight Studies* Tamiris; *Hypocrisy* Tamiris; *Twentieth Century Bacchante* Tamiris

Piano, Felix Petyrek

First Post-European Trip Concert

Apr 7 1929   New York: Martin Beck Theatre   Presented by New Art Circle as a Benefit for the New School for Social Research

Harmony in Athletics Tamiris; *Hypocrisy* Tamiris; *Twentieth Century Bacchante* Tamiris; *Three Negro Spirituals: Nobody Knows de Trouble I See* Tamiris, *Swing Low, Sweet Chariot* (Tamiris / arr J. R. Johnson) Tamiris and *Joshua Fit de Battle ob Jericho* Tamiris; *Prize Fight Studies* Tamiris; *Popular Rhythms* (Tamiris / W. C. Handy) Tamiris; *Dance of the City* (Tamiris / siren) Tamiris; *Impressions of the Bull Ring* Tamiris; *American Serenade No 1* and *American Serenade No 2* Tamiris; *Revolutionary March* (Tamiris / percussions) Tamiris; *1929 [1927]* Tamiris

Piano, Louis Horst; costumes, Tamiris; tympany, J. P. Butty; decoration for *1929*, Juan Oliver

Early Concert Years, 1927-1929

Popular Demand Program

Apr 14 1929 mat New York: Cort Theatre Presented by I. Robert Broder

Harmony in Athletics Tamiris; *Twentieth Century Bacchante* Tamiris; *Revolutionary March* Tamiris; *Impressions of the Bull Ring* Tamiris; *American Serenade No 1* and *American Serenade No 2* Tamiris; *Portrait of a Lady* Tamiris; *Prize Fight Studies* Tamiris; *Circus Sketches* Tamiris; *Hypocrisy* Tamiris; *Dance of the City* Tamiris; *Three Negro Spirituals: Nobody Knows de Trouble I See, Swing Low, Sweet Chariot* and *Joshua Fit de Battle ob Jericho* Tamiris

Piano, Louis Horst; tympani, J. P. Butty; saxophone, Mr. Hanold; costumes, Tamiris

Private Program for American Woman's Association

Apr 29 1929 eve New York: Assembly Room, 353 W 57 St
Master of Ceremonies: Miss Anne Morgan

Part I
Louise Arnoux, Soprano [1]

Part II
Tamiris in a Group of Modern Dances: *Impressions of the Bull Ring* Tamiris; *Portrait of a Lady* Tamiris; *Negro Spirituals: Nobody Knows de Trouble I See, Swing Low, Sweet Chariot* and *Joshua Fit de Battle ob Jericho* Tamiris

Piano, Louis Horst

Fiesta

History: Opened Sept 17 1929 New York: Garrick Theatre
Closed after 39 performances

Production details: Production, Experimental Theatre, Inc, Provincetown Playhouse at the Garrick Theatre; book, Michael Gold; direction, James Light; settings, Cleon Throckmorton; incidental dances arranging and direction, Tamiris; costumes, Nettie Duff Reade

Cast: Charles McCarthy Jr as Chato, Allen Nagle as Pablo, Harold Garry as Tomas, Edward Segal as Ignacio, Arnold Mirante as Isidro, Paul Dorn as An Old Peon, Martin Glee as A Peon, Ruth Chorpenning as Rafaela, David Fields as Aurelio, William Martin as Miguel, Jack La Rue as Don Felipe, Beverly Sitgreaves as Dona Luisa, Warren Colston as Don Jesus, Carl Benton Reid as Don Enrique, Virginia Venable as Guadalupe, George Tobias as Santiago, Keith Stillman as Uncle Pepe, David De Sisto as Amador, Josef Lazarovici as Sheriff, Virginia Rose as Tombola Woman, Lillian Okun as Juanita and Sophia Delza as A Dancing Girl

Dancers: Anita Case, Brana Ghorn, Esther Junger, Darly Urritia and Malie Urritia

Fiesta Ensemble: Leon S. Birnbaum, Ralph K. Fagin, Anthony Grey, Sidney Kline, Kemble Knight, Donald McHenry, Henry Petersilie, Philip Roll, Albert Rosen, Miriam Ross and Benjamin Taly

Scenes: Act I, The Main Room of Rancho la Loma; II, The Same, a Month later; III, The Plaza of the Town; IV, Scene 1, A place in the woods and Scene 2, same as Act I

---

[1] Program of French and American Folk Music: I (in Alsatian Costume) Songs *La Perneto* (Duhamel), *Aubade* (Leo Pol Morin), *Chanson de quete* (Maurice Emmanuel) and *Rigaudon* (Richard Hageman); II Four Bayou Ballads (in Negro Boy Costume) including *Ah! Suzette chere, Voyez piti milate la, Pauv' piti Momzell' Zizi* and *En avant Grenadiers* (Kurt Schindler)

2 The Experimental Years, 1930–1933

PRECARIOUSLY ESTABLISHED as a concert dancer by the end of 1929 but obviously burdened by the problems of putting on individual programs, Tamiris approached other concert artists who were having similar financial problems. She proposed the Dance Repertory Theatre, an administrative organization whereby four of them would band together to give a series of their individual works each season at a common time and a common theatre with a single staff. Overwhelmed by her logic and enthusiasm, Martha Graham, Doris Humphrey, and Charles Weidman joined with her for two seasons, winters 1930 and 1931 (Agnes de Mille appeared during the second year) with Louis Horst as Musical Director. Evidence shows that honest differences of opinion scuttled the project, but also personal egos of artists could not tolerate a supra-organization that might detract from their fragile statures or deflect their great destinies. The enterprise petered out even though it had been financially viable. Disappointed by this attempt at general cooperation for recognition of this dance only now achieving enough entity to be given a name, Tamiris turned inward to the specific matter of her own "Group."

Here, too, Tamiris had a different vision. Rather than imposing her own technique or style upon her individual dancers, she concentrated upon them as individuals. One soon could identify a Graham dancer or a Humphrey dancer, just as one always had been able to identify a ballet dancer. No one could find a Tamiris dancer so marked. In developing her group, she concentrated on the movements of the individuals within it rather than imposed her own style upon them. Her practice was based on her belief that the body itself knew how to move. It did not require someone else to tell it to breathe, contract, or fall. A suggestion from her as the leader of the group was enough to cause its individual members to move with honesty and clarity in expressing the suggestion. High-flying theories were superfluous. Group expression developed out of the interaction of these bodies; it came by organic necessity, compounded by space, after a common action or image had been given by suggestion.

If any philosophical accent emerged in her existential approach, it was that life was conflict. Any dance that did not show the power and strength inherent in life itself was no longer meaningful. She sought and found movement, essentially primitive, which had the torso as its center, the face and limbs fringes of outflow which linked the motion of the dancer and his meaning to the outer world. She began with basic, universal rhythm; she let it carry the body where and how it would.

The Dance Repertory experiment failed; the Tamiris Group grew;

The Experimental Years, 1930-1933

a third experiment Tamiris wrestled with during these maturing years was determining to modern dance itself. Since she began with rhythm, the rhythm of the body, not of music, accompaniment, musical or other, had to follow. She had always used unusual accompaniment; she had dispensed with it altogether in her early solo *The Queen Walks in the Garden*. Now she made the dancers become integrally involved in making their own accompaniment. Her experiments, not always effective, began with a two-part *Triangle Dance*, in which the dancers demarcated accents of movement with differently tuned and sized triangles which they carried and hit. Another dance similarly utilized woodblocks, and a solo moved with a cymbal. Gourd rattles were more successful in *Gris-Gris Ceremonial*, but her artistic statement of this point of view was *Mourning Ceremonial*. With unerring impulse, her dancers as they moved beat their elbows on small drums carried in their hands. The combination of the sound of the savage drums, the sight of the ceremonial costumes, and the feeling of inner compulsion produced an effective dance. Most importantly, however, Tamiris had proved for herself that dance as an art form could exist without the domination of music. She was not the only one to develop this basic tenet of all good concert dance, but she was one of those who at this time found it necessary to show again that dance is an independent art, with accompaniment (musical or otherwise), costume, and decor growing out of it.

Tamiris, the great exponent of the physicality of things, found it necessary, during this period, to deal with the abstract per se in dance. For a time she deserted her robust, four-square methods of moving, for thinness of material and vagueness of intention. Solos like *Eroica* and *Transition*, with fragmentary bits of static movement strung together, were painful to observe. John Martin wished she would soon cut loose from this phase of her modernity and dash about the stage with her sheer loveliness of movement, as in *Mirage*, or face a universal theme with her clarity of form from theme, as in *Dirge*. She soon did so, for she was then beginning an association with the Group Theatre which had an emphasis on human motivation. During these transitional years, she seemed to be clearing the way for coming statements on social themes welling up in her.

As in 1929 she had not confined her work to the concert stage but had ventured into the theatre of plays by choreographing a scene for the three-act *Fiesta*, so in 1933 she essayed the vastness of an auditorium as opposed to the intimacy of the concert stage. She appeared at Lewisohn Stadium and Radio City Music Hall, both mammoth panoramic stages which required an approach of their own. In these, she had to concentrate on pleasing a large popular audience. Under-surface intention, she soon learned, had to be sacrificed, but not clarity. Any tendency toward self-expression was soon curbed in an environment that required universality as well as entertainment. Both were enriching and successful experiences for the growing artist.

In one area, Tamiris never had to experiment. She was always superb in her expression of Negro spirituals in movement. Her predilection was based on their intricate rhythms, first of all. Innately, artistically, spiritually, temperamentally rhythmical, she was never false in the world of the Negro spiritual. In addition, her sympathy for the oppressed human being was a part of her very bones. But mostly, the uninhibited nature, the extemporaneous air, the free-flowing life of the Negro as expressed in their songs appealed to her love of the impromptu and the unpremeditated. Her suite of *Negro Spirituals*, performed with from one to nine different songs of varying intensities of feeling, were always genuine expressions of the human being that was Tamiris.

The Dance Repertory Theatre, First Year

Martha Graham, Doris Humphrey, Charles Weidman, Tamiris; Musical Director, Louis Horst

Jan 5 1930   eve   New York: Maxine Elliott's Theatre   Presented by The Actor-Managers, Inc

Part I
Martha Graham and Group [2]

Part II
Impressions of the Bull Ring Tamiris; *Twentieth Century Bacchante* Tamiris; *Portrait of a Lady* Tamiris; *Dance of the City* Tamiris; *Three Negro Spirituals: Nobody Knows de Trouble I See, Swing Low, Sweet Chariot* and *Joshua Fit de Battle ob Jericho* Tamiris

Piano, Louis Horst; saxophone, Jascha Gurewich; costumes, Tamiris

Part III
Doris Humphrey, Charles Weidman and the Concert Group [3]

---

[2] *Danse* (Graham / Honegger) Graham; *Deux Valses Sentimentales* (Graham / Ravel) Graham; *Four Insincerities: Petulance, Remorse, Politeness* and *Vivacity* (Graham / Prokofieff) Graham; *Adolescense* (Graham / Hindemith) Graham; *Fragments* (a) *Tragedy*, (b) *Comedy* (Graham / Louis Horst) Graham; *Heretic* (Graham / Old Breton song) Graham and group
  Piano, Louis Horst; flute, Hugo Bergamasco; Personal manager, Daniel Mayer
  Group members: Virginia Briton, Hortense Bunsick, Louise Creston, Irene Emery, Martha Hill, Betty Macdonald, Lillian Ray, Kitty Reese, Mary Rivoire, Ethel Rudy, Bessie Schoenberg, Lillian Shapiro, Gertrude Shurr, Anna Sokolov, Sylvia Wasserstrom and Ruth White

[3] *Concerto in A Minor* (Humphrey / Grieg) Humphrey and ensemble; *Japanese Actor (17th Century)* (Weidman / Louis Horst) Weidman; *Life of the Bee* (Humphrey / droning chorus) Humphrey, Cleo Atheneos and ensemble; *The Minstrels* (Weidman / Debussy) Weidman with John Glenn and Eugene Le Sieur; *Etude No 12* (Humphrey / Scriabin) Humphrey and Weidman
  Piano, Louis Horst; Personal manager, Wm. C. Gassner
  Ensemble members: Ruth Allred, Cleo Atheneos, Rose Chrystol, Justine Douglas, Evelyn Fields, Leja Gorska, Ernestine Hennoch, Letitia Ide, Eleanor King, Virginia Landreth, Dorothy Lathrop, Katherine Manning, Sylvia Manning, Rose Yasgour, John Glenn and Eugene Le Sieur
  On Monday evening, January 6 1930, the Dance Repertory Theatre presented Doris Humphrey, Charles Weidman and the Concert Group in the following program:
  A Salutation to the Depths (Humphrey-Weidman / Rudhyar) Humphrey and Weidman; *Water Study* (Humphrey /   ) ensemble; *Preludes* (Weidman / George Gershwin) Weidman; *The Call* and *Breath of Fire* (Humphrey / Rudhyar) Humphrey; *Drama of Motion: Processional (Design), Transition and Interlude (Rhythm),* and *Conclusion (Contrasting Qualities)* (Humphrey /   ) Humphrey and ensemble; *Air on a Ground Bass* (Humphrey / Purcell) Humphrey and Weidman; *The Tumbler of our Lady* (Weidman / Respighi) Weidman, Eu-

The Dance Repertory Theatre, First Year

Tamiris, assisted by 3 dancers

Jan 7 1930   eve   New York: Maxine Elliott's Theatre   Presented by The Actor-Managers, Inc

Harmony in Athletics Tamiris; *Suite: Peasant Rhythms* Tamiris, *Play Dance* (Tamiris / Stravinsky) Tamiris, and *Romantic* (Tamiris / Stravinsky) Tamiris; *Impressions of the Bull Ring* Tamiris; *Hypocrisy* Tamiris; *Lull* (Tamiris / cymbal) Tamiris; *Sentimental Dance* (Tamiris / Copland) Tamiris; *Three Negro Spirituals: Nobody Knows de Trouble I See, Swing Low, Sweet Chariot,* and *Joshua Fit de Battle ob Jericho* Tamiris; *Revolutionary March* Tamiris; *Dirge* (Tamiris / John Powell) Tamiris; *Triangle Dance* (Tamiris / triangles) Tamiris with Emma, Etille and Freda

Piano, Louis Horst assisted in *Dirge* by Ellen Edwards, Ruth Gordon, Pauline Lawrence, Otto Luening, Dini de Remer, and Mr Schlein; tympani, Alfred Friese; saxophone, Jascha Gurewich; lighting, Livingston Platt; costumes, Tamiris.[4]

---

gene Le Sieur and ensemble; *Suite: Poem No 2* (Humphrey-Weidman / Scriabin) Humphrey and Weidman, *Study* (Weidman / Scriabin) and *Etude No 12* (Humphrey-Weidman / Scriabin) Humphrey and Weidman; *The Marionette Theatre* (Weidman / Prokofieff) Weidman with Sylvia Manning, John Glenn and Eugene Le Sieur; *Choreographic Waltz* (Humphrey-Weidman / Ravel) Humphrey and Weidman.

Ensemble members: Ruth Allred, Cleo Atheneos, Rose Chrystol, Justine Douglas, Evelyn Fields, Leja Gorska, Eleanor King, Virginia Landreth, Dorothy Lathrop, Sylvia Manning, Katherine Manning, Rose Yascour, Charles Bougner, George Esterowitz, John Glenn, Charles Lasky and Eugene Le Sieur

Piano, Louis Horst, D. Rudhyar and Pauline Lawrence; Personal manager, William C. Gassner

[4] On Wednesday evening, January 8 1930, the Dance Repertory Theatre presented Martha Graham and her Dance Group in the following program:

Dance (Graham / Honegger) Graham; *Immigrant: Steerage* and *Strike* (Graham / Slavenski) Graham; *Four Insincerities: Petulance, Remorse, Politeness,* and *Vivacity* (Graham / Prokofieff) Graham; *Adolescence* (Graham / Hindemith) Graham; *Prelude to a Dance (Counterpoint No. 1)* (Graham / Honegger) group; *Two Chants: Futility* and *Ecstatic Song* (Graham / Krenek) Graham; *Lamentation* (Graham / Kodaly) Graham; *Portals* (Graham / Carl Ruggles) Graham and group; *Harlequinade: Pessimist* and *Optimist* (Graham / Toch) Graham; *Sketches from the People: Monotony, Supplication* and *Requiem* (Graham / Krein) group; *Fragments: Tragedy* and *Comedy* (Graham / Louis Horst) Graham; *Heretic* (Graham / Old Breton song) Graham and group

Piano, Louis Horst; flute, Hugo Bergamasco; music for *Portals,* members of The Conductorless Orchestra; lighting, Livingston Platt; Personal manager, Daniel Mayer

Members of group: Virginia Briton, Hortense Bunsick, Louise Creston, Irene Emery, Martha Hill, Betty Macdonald, Lillian Ray, Kitty Reese, Mary Rivoire, Ethel Rudy, Bessie Schoenberg, Lillian Shapiro, Gertrude Shurr, Anna Sokolov, Sylvia Wasserstrom and Ruth White

On Thursday evening, January 9 1930, the Dance Repertory Theatre presented Doris Humphrey, Charles Weidman and the Concert Group in the following program:

Salutation to the Depths (Humphrey-Weidman / Rudhyar) Humphrey and Weidman; *Three Studies: Diffidence, Annoyance, Rage* (Weidman / Honegger) Weidman; *Drama of Motion: Processional (Design), Transition and Interlude (Rhythm)* and *Conclusion (Contrasting Qualities)* (Humphrey /   ) Humphrey and ensemble; *The Call* and *Breath of Fire* (Humphrey / Rudhyar) Humphrey; *Color Harmony* (Humphrey / Clifford Vaughn) Weidman, Leja Gorska and ensemble; *Air on a Ground Bass* (Humphrey / Purcell) Humphrey and Weidman; *The Marionette Theatre* (Weidman / Prokofieff) Weidman, Sylvia Manning, John Glenn and Eugene Le Sieur; *Descent* (Humphrey / Adolph Weiss) Humphrey; *The Conspirator* (Weidman /   ) Weidman and ensemble; *Scherzo* (Weidman / Borodin) Weidman; *Concerto in A Minor* (Humphrey / Grieg) Humphrey and ensemble

The Dance Repertory Theatre, First Year

Tamiris, assisted by 3 dancers

Jan 10 1930 eve   New York: Maxine Elliott's Theatre   Presented by The Actor-Managers, Inc

American Serenade Tamiris; *Suite: Peasant Rhythms, Play Dance* and *Romantic* Tamiris; *Prize Fight Studies* Tamiris; *Hypocrisy* Tamiris; *Lull* Tamiris; *Sentimental Dance* Tamiris; *Three Negro Spirituals: Nobody Knows de Trouble I See, Swing Low, Sweet Chariot* and *Joshua Fit de Battle ob Jericho* Tamiris; *Revolutionary March* Tamiris; *Dirge* Tamiris; *Triangle Dance* Tamiris with Emma, Etille and Freda

Piano, Louis Horst assisted in *Dirge* by Ellen Edwards, Ruth Gordon, Pauline Lawrence, Otto Luening, Dini de Remer and Mr Schlein; tympani, Alfred Friese; saxophone, Jascha Gurewich; lighting, Livingston Platt; costumes, Tamiris

The Dance Repertory Theatre, First Year

Martha Graham, Doris Humphrey, Charles Weidman, Tamiris; Musical Director, Louis Horst

Jan 11 1930 mat   New York: Maxine Elliott's Theatre   Presented by The Actor-Managers, Inc

Part I
Martha Graham and Group[5]

Part II
Revolutionary March Tamiris; *Three Negro Spirituals: Nobody Knows de Trouble I See, Swing Low, Sweet Chariot* and *Joshua Fit de Battle ob Jericho* Tamiris; *Dance of the City* Tamiris; *Hypocrisy* Tamiris; *Dirge* Tamiris; *Triangle Dance* Tamiris with Emma, Etille and Freda

Piano, Louis Horst; tympany, Alfred Friese; saxophone, Jascha Gurewich; costumes, Tamiris

Part III
Doris Humphrey, Charles Weidman and the Concert Group[6]

Piano, Louis Horst and D. Rudhyar; flute, Maurice Sackett; Personal manager, William C. Gassner

Members of ensemble: Ruth Allred, Cleo Atheneos, Rose Chrystol, Justine Douglas, Evelyn Fields, Margaret Gardner, Leja Gorska, Ilse Gronau, Ernestine Hennoch, Letitia Ide, Eleanor King, Virginia Landreth, Dorothy Lathrop, Katherine Manning, Sylvia Manning, Betty Schlaffer, Rose Yasgour, John Glenn, Arthur Muller and Eugene Le Sieur

[5] *Danse* (Graham / Honegger) Graham; *Deux Valses Sentimentales* (Graham / Ravel) Graham; *Danse Languide* (Graham / Scriabin) Evelyn, Betty and Rosina; *Tanagra* (Graham / Satie) Graham; *Fragments: Tragedy* and *Comedy* (Graham / Horst) Graham; *Heretic* (Graham / Old Breton song) Graham and group

Piano, Louis Horst; flute, Hugo Bergamasco; lighting, Livingston Platt; Personal manager, Daniel Mayer Concert Direction

Members of the group: Virginia Briton, Hortense Bunsick, Louise Creston, Irene Emery, Martha Hill, Betty Macdonald, Lillian Ray, Kitty Reese, Mary Rivoire, Ethel Rudy, Bessie Schoenberg, Lillian Shapiro, Gertrude Shurr, Anna Sokolov, Sylvia Wasserstrom and Ruth White

[6] *A Salutation to the Depths* (Humphrey-Weidman / Rudhyar) Humphrey and Weidman; *Water Study* (Humphrey /   ) ensemble; *The Call* and *Breath of Fire* (Humphrey / Rudhyar) Humphrey; *Passion* and *Compassion* (Weidman / Satie) Weidman; *La Valse* [*Choreographic Waltz*] (Humphrey-Weidman / Ravel) Humphrey, Weidman and ensemble

Piano, Louis Horst, D. Rudhyar and Pauline Lawrence; Personal manager, William C. Gassner

Ensemble members: Ruth Allred, Cleo Atheneos, Rose Chrystol, Justine Douglas, Evelyn

The Dance Repertory Theatre, First Year

Martha Graham, Tamiris, and Doris Humphrey and Charles Weidman[7]

Jan 12 1930   Sun eve   New York: Maxine Elliott's Theatre   Presented by The Actor-Managers, Inc

Part I
Martha Graham and Group[8]

Part II
Sentimental Dance Tamiris; *Three Negro Spirituals: Nobody Knows de Trouble I See, Swing Low, Sweet Chariot* and *Joshua Fit de Battle ob Jericho* Tamiris; *Dance of the City* Tamiris; *Dirge* Tamiris; *Triangle Dance* Tamiris with Emma, Etille and Freda

Piano, Genevieve Pitot

Part III
Doris Humphrey, Charles Weidman and the Concert Group[9]

Fields, Margaret Gardner, Leja Gorska, Ilse Gronau, Ernestine Hennoch, Letitia Ide, Eleanor King, Virginia Landreth, Dorothy Lathrop, Katherine Manning, Sylvia Manning, Betty Schlaffer, Rose Yasgour, Charles Boughner, George Esterowitz, John Glenn, Charles Lasky, Arthur Miller and Eugene Le Sieur

On Saturday evening, January 11 1930, the Dance Repertory Theatre presented Martha Graham and her Dance Group in the following program:

Dance (Graham / Honegger) Graham; *Deux Valses Sentimentales* (Graham / Ravel) Graham; *Moment Rustica* (Graham / Poulenc) group; *Adolescence* (Graham / Hindemith) Graham; *Vision of the Apocalypse: Toil, Famine, Ruthlessness, Pestilence, Mourning, Prayer* and *Judgment* (Graham / Reutter) group; *Fragments: Tragedy* and *Comedy* (Graham / Louis Horst) Graham; *Lamentation* (Graham / Kodaly) Graham; *Project in Movement for a Divine Comedy* (Graham /   ) Graham and group; *Two Chants: Futility* and *Ecstatic Song* (Graham / Krenek) Graham; *Sketches from the People: Monotony, Supplication* and *Requiem* (Graham / Krein) group; *Harlequinade: Pessimist* and *Optimist* (Graham / Toch) Graham; *Heretic* (Graham / Old Breton song) Graham and group

Piano, Louis Horst; lighting, Livingston Platt; Personal manager, Daniel Mayer Concert Direction

Members of group: Virginia Briton, Hortense Bunsick, Louise Creston, Irene Emery, Martha Hill, Betty Macdonald, Lillian Ray, Kitty Reese, Mary Rivoire, Ethel Rudy, Bessie Schoenberg, Lillian Shapiro, Gertrude Shurr, Anna Sokolov, Sylvia Wasserstrom and Ruth White

[7] On January 13 1930, in a review of this program, the New York *Times* wrote, "The only blemish on the evening, and that a considerable one, was the illness of Louis Horst, the musical director and accompanist at all the other performances. Four pianists were required to fill his place.... In spite of their excellent emergency service, Mr. Horst's presence was missed both by dancers and audience."

[8] *Danse* (Graham / Honegger) Graham; *Moment Rustica* (Graham / Poulenc) group; *Lamentation* (Graham / Kodaly) Graham; *Project in Movement for a Divine Comedy* (Graham /   ) Graham and group;) *Heretic* (Graham/ Old Breton song) Graham and group

Piano, Ruth Gordon and Dini de Remer

Members of the group: Virginia Briton, Hortense Bunsick, Louise Creston, Irene Emery, Martha Hill, Betty Macdonald, Lillian Ray, Kitty Reese, Mary Rivoire, Ethel Rudy, Bessie Schoenberg, Lillian Shapiro, Gertrude Shurr, Anna Sokolov, Sylvia Wasserstrom and Ruth White

[9] *Salutation to the Depths* (Humphrey-Weidman / Rudhyar) Humphrey and Weidman; *Drama of Motion* (Humphrey /   ) Humphrey and ensemble; *Descent into a Dangerous Place* (Humphrey / Adolph Weiss) Humphrey; *The Marionette Theatre* (Weidman / Prokofieff) Weidman, Sylvia Manning, John Glenn and Eugene Le Sieur; *The Conspirator* (Weidman /   ) Weidman and ensemble; *Air on a Ground Bass* (Humphrey / Purcell) Humphrey and Weidman

Piano, Pauline Lawrence

The Dance Repertory Theatre, Second Year

Doris Humphrey and her Concert Group; Divertissements by Agnes de Mille assisted by Warren Leonard, by Charles Weidman and his Group and by Tamiris' Group; Musical Director, Louis Horst

Feb 1 1931   eve   New York: Craig Theatre

[*March* (Humphrey / Tcherepnine) Humphrey's concert group];[10] *Woodblock Dance* (Tamiris / woodblocks) Sylvia Averbuck, Dvo Seron, Ida Soyer and Rose Warshaw; [*Ballet Class (Degas Study)* (De Mille / Strauss) De Mille; *Dances of Women* (Humphrey / Rudhyar) Humphrey and concert group; *The Shakers* (Humphrey / accordion, drum and voice) Humphrey's concert group; *Ringside* (Weidman / Sargent) Charles Lasky and Jose Limon]; *Revolutionary March* (Tamiris / percussions) Sylvia Avebuck, Ethel Axel, Freda Granett, Beatrice Schindler, Ida Tarvin and Rose Warshaw; [*May Day* (De Mille / Beethoven) De Mille and Leonard; *The Marionette Theatre* (Weidman / Prokofieff) Weidman with Sylvia Manning, George Steares and Eugene Le Sieur; *Can-can* (De Mille / Offenbach) De Mille and Leonard]

Piano, Louis Horst; costumes, Tamiris; tympani, Perrin; lighting, A. Feder

The Dance Repertory Theatre, Second Year

Tamiris and her Group; Divertissements by Martha Graham's Group, by Agnes de Mille, and by Charles Weidman and Group

Feb 3 1931   eve   New York: Craig Theatre

[*Ringside* (Weidman / Winthrop Sargeant) Weidman's group[11]; *Julia Dances* (De Mille / Thomas Weelkes, arr Louis Horst) De Mille]; *Olympus Americanus—A 20th Cen-*

Members of ensemble: Ruth Allred, Cleo Atheneos, Rose Chrystol, Justine Douglas, Evelyn Fields, Margaret Gardner, Leja Gorska, Ilse Gronau, Ernestine Hennoch, Letitia Ide, Eleanor King, Virginia Landreth, Dorothy Lathrop, Katherine Manning, Sylvia Manning, Betty Schlaffer, Rose Yasgour, John Glenn, Arthur Muller and Eugene Le Sieur

[10] Humphrey's concert group members: Sylvia Manning, Evelyn Fields, Rose Yasgour, Cleo Atheneos, Ruth Allred, Celia Rauch, Dorothy Lathrop, Katherine Manning, Rose Crystol, Eleanor King, Ada Korvin, Letitia Ide, Ernestine Henoch, Virginia Landreth, Helen Strumlauf, Charles Lasky and Jose Limon

On Monday evening, February 2 1931, the Dance Repertory Theatre presented Martha Graham and her Dance Group in the following program:

Dance (Graham / Honegger) Graham; *Lamentation* (Graham / Kodaly) Graham; *Moment Rustica* (Graham / Poulenc) group; *Two Primitive Canticles: Ave* and *Salve* (Graham / Villa-Lobos) Graham; *Primitive Mysteries: Hymn to the Virgin, Crucifixus* and *Hosanna* (Graham / Louis Horst) Graham and group; *Adolescence* (Graham / Hindemith) Graham; *Project in Movement for a Divine Comedy* (Graham /   ) Graham and group; *Rhapsodics* (Graham / Bartok) Graham; *Bacchanale* (Graham / Wallingford Riegger) Graham and group; *Dolorosa* (Graham / Villa-Lobos) Graham; *Harlequinade: Pessimist* and *Optimist* (Graham / Toch) Graham; *Heretic* (Graham / Old Breton song) Graham and group

Piano, Louis Horst and Dini de Remer; flute, Hugo Bergamasco; oboe, William Sergeant

Members of the group: Lillian Shapero, Grace Cornell, Mary Rivoire, Joane Woodruff, Ruth White, Gertrude Shurr, Louise Creston, Anna Sokolov, Lillian Ray, Ethel Rudy, Hortense Burkin, Virginia Briton, Martha Todd, Pauline Nelson, Bessie Schoenberg, Ailes Gilmour, Dorothy Bird and Georgia Graham

[11] Weidman's group members: Charles Laskey, Jose Limon, George Steares and Eugene Le Sieur

The Experimental Years, 1930-1933

tury Ballet Themes: *Basking in the Sun, Dance on an Ancient Theme (Priapic Ritual), Tempo, Dance to Hermes and Aphrodite, The Races* and *Triumphant* ("The work is an attempt to weld the contemporary spirit with the classic. There is no plot, no superimposed story, no narrative in the sense of the libretto of the traditional ballet d'action. The Ideology evolves out of the movement itself. The themes in the ballet mark the accents of life in ancient Greece and in our twentieth century.") (Tamiris / Copland) Tamiris with Sylvia Avebuck, Ethel Axel, Elizabeth Baker, Sydne Becker, Freda Granett, Gladys Rappaport, Beatrice Schindler, Dvo Seron, Ida Soyer, Ruth Sunenshine, Ida Tarvin and Rose Warshaw; [*Moment Rustica* (Graham / Poulenc) Graham's group][12] *Dirge* Tamiris ['49 (De Mille / Cowboy tunes arr Guion) De Mille; *Sketches of the People: Monotony, Supplication* and *Requiem* (Graham / Krein) Graham's group;[12] *The Marionette Theatre* Weidman / Prokofieff) Weidman's group];[11] *Impressions of the Bull Ring* Tamiris

Piano, Louis Horst assisted by Genevieve Pitot; costumes, Tamiris; orchestra conductor, Louis Horst[13]

---

[12] Graham's group members: Lillian Shapero, Grace Cornell, Mary Rivoire, Joane Woodruff, Ruth White, Gertrude Shurr, Louise Creston, Anna Sokolov, Lillian Ray, Ethel Rudy, Hortense Burkin, Virginia Briton, Martha Todd, Pauline Nelson, Bessie Schoenberg, Ailes Gilmour, Dorothy Bird and Georgia Graham

[13] On Wednesday evening February 4 1931 the Dance Repertory Theatre Doris Humphrey-Charles Weidman and their Concert Groups in the following program:

Salutation to the Depths (Humphrey-Weidman / Rudhyar) Humphrey and Weidman; *Gigue* (Humphrey / Bach) Humphrey; *Danse Profane* (Weidman / Debussy) Weidman; *Drama of Motion: Processional, Transition and Interlude* and *Conclusion* (Humphrey /   ) Humphrey and concert group; *Air on a Ground Bass* (Humphrey / Purcell) and *Burlesca* (Weidman / Bossi) Humphrey and Weidman; *Steel and Stone* (Weidman / Cowell) Weidman with Charles Laskey and Jose Limon; *The Shakers* (Humphrey / accordion, drum and voice) Humphrey and her concert group; *Lake at Evening* and *Night Winds* (Humphrey / Griffes) Humphrey; *Dances of Women* (Humphrey / Rudhyar) Humphrey and her concert group; *Scherzo* (Weidman / Borodin) Weidman; *Descent into a Dangerous Place* (Humphrey / Weiss) Humphrey; *Choreographic Waltz* (Humphrey-Weidman / Ravel) Humphrey, Weidman and Humphrey's concert group

Piano, Louis Horst assisted by Pauline Lawrence and D. Rudyhar

Humphrey's group members: Sylvia Manning, Evelyn Fields, Rose Yasgour, Cleo Atheneos, Ruth Allred, Celia Rauch, Dorothy Lathrop, Katherine Manning, Rose Chrystol, Eleanor King, Ada Korvin, Letitia Ide, Ernestine Henoch, Virginia Landreth and Helen Strumlauf

Weidman's group members: Charles Laskey, Jose Limon, George Steares and Eugene Le Sieur

On Thursday evening, February 5 1931, the Dance Repertory Theatre presented Agnes George de Mille, assisted by Warren Leonard, with divertissements by Doris Humphrey's Concert Group and Martha Graham's Group, in the following program:

Theme and Variations (De Mille / Hayden) De Mille; *Burgomaster's Branle* (De Mille / Ancient Dutch airs arr Roentgen) De Mille and Leonard; *The Cries of London* (De Mille / arr William Irwin) De Mille; *March* (Humphrey / Tcherepnine) Humphrey's concert group; *Tryout* (De Mille / Ray Henderson) De Mille; *The Shakers* (Humphrey / accordion, drum and voice) Humphrey's concert group; *Cafe Dancer* (De Mille / Kurdish tunes arr Sven van Hallberg) De Mille; *The Parvenues* (De Mille / Strauss-Waldteufel) De Mille and Leonard; *Sketches of the People: Monotony, Supplication* and *Requiem* (Graham / Krein) Graham's group; *Gigue from Fifth French Suite* (De Mille / Bach) De Mille; *Nocturne* (Leonard / Selim Palmgren) De Mille and Leonard; *Moment Rustica* (Graham / Poulenc) Graham's group; *May Day* (De Mille / Beethoven) De Mille and Leonard; *Armistice Day* (De Mille / William Irwin) De Mille

Piano, Louis Horst and William Irwin; costumes, De Mille

Humphrey's concert group members: Sylvia Manning, Evelyn Fields, Rose Yasgour, Cleo Atheneos, Ruth Allred, Celia Rauch, Dorothy Lathrop, Katherine Manning, Rose Crystol, Eleanor King, Ada Korvin, Letitia Ide, Ernestine Henoch, Virginia Landreth and Helen Strumlauf

Graham's group members: Lillian Shapero, Grace Cornell, Mary Rivoire, Joane Woodruff, Ruth White, Gertrude Shurr, Louise Creston, Anna Sokolov, Lillian Ray, Ethel Rudy, Hortense

The Dance Repertory Theatre, Second Year

Martha Graham, assisted by her Dance Group; Divertissements by Doris Humphrey's Concert Group, by Agnes de Mille assisted by Warren Leonard, and by Tamiris' Group

Feb 6 1931   eve   New York: Craig Theatre

[*Bacchanale* (Graham / Wallingford Riegger) Graham and group[14]; *Adolescence* (Graham / Hindemith) Graham; *Rhapsodics: Song, Interlude* and *Dance* (Graham / Bartok) Graham; *Two Primitive Canticles: Ave* and *Salve* (Graham / Villa-Lobos) Graham; *Primitive Mysteries: Hymn to the Virgin, Crucifixus* and *Hosanna* (Graham / Louis Horst) Graham and group]; *Dance to Hermes and Aphrodite,* from *Olympus Americanus* Sylvia Averbuck, Ethel Axel, Elizabeth Baker, Sydne Becker, Freda Granett, Gladys Rappaport, Beatrice Schindler, Dvo Seron, Ida Soyer, Ruth Sunenshine, Ida Tarvin and Rose Warshaw;

[*Water Study* (Humphrey /   ) Humphrey's concert group;[15] *Tryout* (De Mille / Ray Henderson) De Mille]; *Woodblock Dance* Sylvia Averbuck, Dvo Seron, Ida Soyer, Rose Warshaw and Ida Tarvin; [*Cafe Dancer* (De Mille / Old Kirdish tunes arr Sven van Hallberg) De Mille]; *Revolutionary March* Sylvia Averbuck, Ethel Axel, Freda Granett, Beatrice Schindler, Dvo Seron, Ida Soyer, Ida Tarvin and Rose Warshaw; [*Can-can* (De Mille / Offenbach) De Mille and Leonard]

Piano, Louis Horst assisted by Genevieve Pitot; tympani, J. Perrin; lighting, A. Feder; costumes, Tamiris[16]

The Dance Repertory Theatre, Second Year

Tamiris and her Group

Feb 7 1931   eve   New York: Craig Theatre

Mirage (Tamiris / S. Palmgren) Tamiris; *South American Dance* (Tamiris / Rodriquez) Tamiris; *Dance of Exuberance* (Tamiris / Nathan Novick) Tamiris; *Tri-*

Burkin, Virginia Briton, Martha Todd, Pauline Nelson, Bessie Schoenberg, Ailes Gilmour and Dorothy Bird

[14] Lillian Shapero, Grace Cornell, Mary Rivoire, Joane Woodruff, Ruth White, Gertrude Shurr, Louise Creston, Anna Sokolov, Lillian Ray, Ethel Rudy, Hortense Burkin, Virginia Briton, Martha Todd, Pauline Nelson, Bessie Schoenberg, Ailes Gilmour, Dorothy Bird and Georgia Graham

[15] Sylvia Manning, Evelyn Fields, Rose Yasgour, Cleo Atheneos, Ruth Allred, Celia Rauch, Dorothy Lathrop, Katherine Manning, Rose Crystol, Eleanor King, Ada Korvin, Letitia Ide, Ernestine Henoch, Virginia Landreth, Helen Strumlauf, Charles Lasky and Jose Limon

[16] On Saturday afternoon, February 7 1931, the Dance Repertory Theatre presented Charles Weidman and his Concert Group, with divertissements by Doris Humphrey's Concert Group, Martha Graham's Group, and Agnes de Mille assisted by Warren Leonard, in the following program:

March (Humphrey / Tcherepnine) Humphrey's concert group; *Stagefright* (De Mille / Delibes) De Mille; *Primitive Mysteries: Hymn to the Virgin, Crucifixus* and *Hosanna* (Graham / Louis Horst) Lillian Shapero and Graham's group; *Civil War* (De Mille / Civil War Song arr Horst) De Mille; *Drama of Motion: Conclusion* (Humphrey /   ) Humphrey's concert group; *The Parvenues* (De Mille / Strauss-Waldteufel) De Mille and Leonard; "The Happy Hypocrite" ("A Fairy Tale for Tired Men" by Max Beerbohm) (Weidman / Herbert Elwell) members from Weidman's and Humphrey's groups

Weidman's concert group members: Darley Fuller, Charles Laskey, Jose Limon, Eugene Le Sieur and George Steares

Humphrey's concert group members: Sylvia Manning, Evelyn Fields, Rose Yasgour, Cleo

The Experimental Years, 1930-1933

angle Dance and Triangle Dance, Part Two (Tamiris / triangles) Tamiris with Sylvia Averbuck, Sydne Becker, Freda Granett, Dvo Seron, Ida Soyer, Ida Tarvin and Rose Warshaw; *Negro Spirituals: Nobody Knows de Trouble I See* Tamiris, *Crucifixion* (Tamiris / arr J. R. Johnson) Tamiris, *Swing Low, Sweet Chariot* Tamiris and *Joshua Fit de Battle ob Jericho* Tamiris; *Olympus Americanus—A Twentieth Century Ballet* Tamiris with Sylvia Averbuck, Ethel Axel, Elizabeth Baker, Sydne Becker, Freda Granett, Gladys Rappaport, Beatrice Schindler, Dvo Seron, Ida Soyer, Ruth Sunenshine, Ida Tarvin and Rose Warshaw

Orchestra conductor, Louis Horst; guitar, W. Salmon; piano, Genevieve Pitot; lighting, A. Feder; costumes, Tamiris

The Dance Repertory Theatre, Second Year

Martha Graham and her Group, Doris Humphrey and her Concert Group, Agnes de Mille assisted by Warren Leonard, Tamiris and her Group, and Charles Weidman and his Group; Musical Director, Louis Horst

Feb 8 1931   mat   New York: Craig Theatre

Part I
Graham and her Group[17]

Part II
Weidman and his Group[18]

Part III
Humphrey and Concert Group[19]

Part IV
Dance of Exuberance Tamiris; *Triangle Dance* and *Triangle Dance, Part Two* Tamiris with Sylvia Averbuck, Sydne Becker, Freda Granett, Dvo Seron, Ida Soyer, Ida Tarvin and Rose Warshaw; *South American Dance* Tamiris; *Negro Spirituals: Nobody Knows de Trouble I See, Crucifixion, Swing Low, Sweet Chariot,* and *Joshua Fit de Battle ob Jericho* Tamiris

Piano, Genevieve Pitot; guitar, W. Salmon; lighting, A. Feder; costumes, Tamiris

Part V
De Mille assisted by Warren Leonard[20]

Atheneos, Ruth Allred, Celia Rauch, Dorothy Lathrop, Katherine Manning, Rose Crystol Eleanor King, Ada Korvin, Letitia Ide, Ernestine Henoch, Virginia Landreth and Helen Strumlauf
[17] *Dance* (Graham / Honegger) Graham; *Harlequinade: Pessimist* and *Optimist* (Graham / Toch) Graham; *Lamentation* (Graham / Kodaly) Graham; *Heretic* (Graham / Old Breton song) Graham and group
   Graham's group members: Lillian Shapero, Grace Cornell, Mary Rivoire, Joane Woodruff, Ruth White, Gertrude Shurr, Louise Creston, Anna Sokolov, Lillian Ray, Ethel Rudy, Hortense Burkin, Virginia Briton, Martha Todd, Pauline Nelson, Bessie Schoenberg, Ailes Gilmour, Dorothy Bird and Georgia Graham
[18] *Steel and Stone* (Weidman / Cowell) Weidman, Charles Laskey and Jose Limon; *The Marionette Theatre* (Weidman / Prokofieff) Wiedman, Sylvia Manning, Eugene Le Sieur and George Steares
[19] *The Shakers* (Humphrey / accordion, drum and voice) Humphrey and concert group
   Humphrey's group members: Sylvia Manning, Evelyn Fields, Rose Yasgour, Cleo Atheneos, Ruth Allred, Celia Rauch, Dorothy Lathrop, Katherine Manning, Rose Crystol, Eleanor King, Ada Korvin, Helen Strumlauf, Letitia Ide, Ernestine Henoch and Virginia Landreth
[20] *May Day* (De Mille / Beethoven) De Mille and Leonard; *Ballet Class (Degas Study)* (De Mille / Strauss) De Mille; *Armistice Day* (De Mille / arr William Irwin) De Mille

Students' Dance Recitals, Washington Irving High School.

Tamiris and her Group

Feb 13 1931   eve   New York: Municipal Auditorium

Triangle Dance and *Triangle Dance, Part Two* Tamiris and group; *Dance of Exuberance* Tamiris; *Mirage* Tamiris; *Woodblock Dance* group; *Hypocrisy* Tamiris; *Two Negro Spirituals: Crucifixion* and *Swing Low, Sweet Chariot* Tamiris; *Twentieth Century Bacchante* Tamiris; *Dance to Hermes and Aphrodite* from *Olympus Americanus* group; *South American Dance* Tamiris; *Dirge* Tamiris; *Revolutionary March* group; *Impressions of the Bull Ring* Tamiris

Group dancers: Sylvia Averbuck, Ethel Axel, Sydne Becker, Freda Granett, Beatrice Schindler, Dvo Seron, Ida Soyer, Ruth Sunenshine, Ida Tarvin and Rose Warshaw

Piano, Genevieve Pitot; guitar, W. Salmon; saxophone, J. Gurewich; tympani, J. Perrin

Premiere of Mourning Ceremonial

Tamiris and her Group

Nov 29 1931   eve   New York: Guild Theatre
Benefit for Miners' Defense Committee

Mirage Tamiris; *Woodblock Dance* group; *Three Negro Spirituals: Nobody Knows de Trouble I See*, *Swing Low, Sweet Chariot* and *Joshua Fit de Battle ob Jericho* Tamiris; *Mourning Ceremonial* (Tamiris / dancers with drums) Tamiris with group; *Dirge* Tamiris; *Eroica* (Tamiris / Alfredo Casella) Tamiris; *Transition* (Tamiris / Alfredo Casella) Tamiris; *Dance on an Ancient Theme* and *Dance to Hermes and Aphrodite* from *Olympus Americanus* group; *South American Dance* Tamiris; *Maenad* (Tamiris / percussion) Tamiris; *Dance for a Holiday* (Tamiris / American folk music) group[21]

Group dancers (?): Sylvia Averbuck, Sydne Becker, Beatrice Schindler, Dvo Seron, Ida Soyer, Ruth Sunenshine, Ida Tarvin and Rose Warshaw

Piano, Genevieve Pitot; percussion, John Waldman and Charles Chancer; guitar, Cornejo; saxophone, Jascha Gurewich

Leading Dance Personalities

Tamiris and Ingeborg Torrup

Jan 27 1932   eve   New York: Roerich Hall

Part I

Dance of Exuberance Tamiris; *Woodblock Dance* group; *Prize Fight Studies* Tamiris; *Dance to Hermes and Aphrodite* from *Olympus Americanus* group; *Maenad* Tamiris; *Mourning Ceremonial* Tamiris with group

Dancers in group: Sydne Becker, Gladys Rappaport, Dvo Seron, Beatrice Schindler, Ida Soyer, Ruth Sunenshine, Ida Tarvin and Rose Warshaw

Piano, Charles Chancer and John Waldman

Part II

Ingeborg Torrup[22]

---

[21] Order of dances and dancers performing individual numbers not known
[22] *Ase's Death* (Torrup / Grieg) Torrup; *Anitra's Dance* (Torrup / Grieg) Torrup; *Allegro Vivace* (Torrup / Grieg) Torrup; *Waltz* (Torrup / Grieg) Torrup; *Ala Mazurka* (Torrup / Scharwenka) Torrup; *Dynamics* (Torrup / H. Walden) Torrup
Piano, Violette Chantal

The Experimental Years, 1930-1933

Students' Dance Recitals, Washington Irving High School

Tamiris and her Group

Feb 20 1932   eve   New York: Municipal Auditorium

Dance of Exuberance Tamiris; *Woodblock Dance* group; *Transition* Tamiris; *Dance to Hermes and Aphrodite* from *Olympus Americanus* group; *Maenad* Tamiris; *Eroica* Tamiris; *Dirge* Tamiris; *South American Dance* Tamiris; *Dance for a Holiday* group; *Impressions of the Bull Ring* Tamiris; *Dance on an Ancient Theme* from *Olympus Americanus* group; *Three Negro Spirituals: Crucifixion, Swing Low, Sweet Chariot* and *Joshua Fit de Battle ob Jericho* Tamiris; *Mourning Ceremonial* Tamiris with group

Dancers in group: Sydne Becker, Gladys Rappaport, Dvo Seron, Beatrice Schindler, Ida Soyer, Ruth Sunenshine, Ida Tarvin and Rose Warshaw

Piano, Genevieve Pitot, Charles Chancer and John Waldman; costumes, Tamiris

New School Dance Recital

Tamiris and her Concert Group

Dec 18 1932   eve   New York: New School for Social Research Auditorium

Mirage Tamiris; *Composition for Group* (Tamiris / J. Slavenski) Sylvia Averbuck, Sydne Becker, Susan Chessen, Ethel Axel, Beatrice Schindler, Ida Soyer, Ruth Sunenshine, Ida Tarvin and Rose Warshaw; *Six Negro Spirituals: Nobody Knows de Trouble I See* Tamiris, *Swing Low, Sweet Chariot* Tamiris, *Crucifixion* Tamiris, *Git on Board Lil Chillen* (Tamiris / arr Lawrence Brown) Tamiris, *Go Down Moses* (Tamiris / arr R. Johnson) Tamiris, *Joshua Fit de Battle ob Jericho* Tamiris; *Gris-Gris Ceremonial* (Tamiris / gourds) Tamiris with Sylvia Averbuck, Sydne Becker, Mollie Horowitz, Susan Chessen, Ethel Axel, Beatrice Schindler, Dvo Seron, Ida Soyer, Ruth Sunenshine and Ida Tarvin; *Eroica* Tamiris; *Mourning Ceremonial* Tamiris with Sylvia Averbuck, Sydne Becker, Beatrice Schindler, Dvo Seron, Ida Soyer, Ruth Sunenshine, Ida Tarvin and Rose Warshaw; *Maenad* Tamiris; *South American Dance* Tamiris; *Dance for a Holiday* Sydne Becker, Beatrice Schindler, Dvo Seron, Ida Tarvin and Rose Warshaw; *Dance of Exuberance* Tamiris

Piano, Yudie Weitzman; percussions, Charles Chancer; costumes, Tamiris

Students' Dance Recitals, Washington Irving High School

Tamiris and her Group

Feb 18 1933   eve   New York: Municipal Auditorium

Dance of Exuberance Tamiris; *Mirage* Tamiris; *Dirge* Tamiris; *Cymbal Dance* (Tamiris / cymbals) Ida Soyer and Ida Tarvin; *Six Negro Spirituals: Nobody Knows de Trouble I See, Swing Low, Sweet Chariot, Crucifixion, Git on Board Lil Chillen, Joshua Fit de Battle ob Jericho* and *Go Down Moses* Tamiris; *Gris-Gris Ceremonial* Tamiris with Sydne Becker, Molly Bornn, Ann Goodson, Freda Granett, Ruth Krauss, Hilda Sheldon, Ida Soyer, Ruth Sunenshine and Ida Tarvin; *Mourning Ceremonial* Tamiris with Sydne Becker, Ida Soyer, Ruth Sunenshine and Ida Tarvin; *Hypocrisy* Tamiris; *South American Dance* Tamiris; *Dance for a Holiday* Sydne Becker, Hilda Sheldon, Ida Soyer, Ruth Sunenshine and Ida Tarvin; *Maenad* Tamiris

Piano, Genevieve Pitot and Samuel Becker; costumes, Tamiris

Cornell University Appearance

Tamiris

May 27 1933   Ithaca, NY: University Theatre   Presented by The Cornell Dramatic Club

Dance of Exuberance Tamiris; *Dirge* Tamiris; *Hypocrisy* Tamiris; *Four Negro Spirituals: Swing Low, Sweet Chariot, Get on Board Lil Chillen, Go Down Moses* and *Joshua Fit de Battle ob Jericho* Tamiris; *Mirage* Tamiris; *Twentieth Century Bacchante* Tamiris; *Solo Figure* from *Gris-Gris Ceremonial* Tamiris; *South American Dance* Tamiris; *Impressions of the Bull Ring* Tamiris

Piano, Genevieve Pitot; costumes, Tamiris

Lewisohn Stadium Concert

Tamiris and Bahama Negro Dancers with Philharmonic Symphony Orchestra

Aug 18–19 1933   eves   New York: Lewisohn Stadium

[*In Old Virginia* (orchestral selection by John Powell); *Crow Dance* Bahama Negro Dancers]; *Five Negro Spirituals: Nobody Knows de Trouble I See, Swing Low, Sweet Chariot, Get on Board Lil Chillun, Go Down Moses* and *Joshua Fit de Battle ob Jericho* Tamiris; [*Dance of the Coconut Grove* Bahama Negro Dancers; *The Bamboula Rhapsodic Dance* (orchestral selection by S. Coleridge-Taylor)]; *Gris-Gris Ceremonial* ("This is a dance based by Tamiris on a Fetich Ritual of West African origin. The 'Gris-Gris' is a charm or amulet in which a protecting spirit is supposed to dwell. Placed in a forest where the ceremonial is enacted, the Image, hewn out of wood, is closely associated with the control of the Powers of Propagation and Black Magic.") (Tamiris /gourds and orchestra) Tamiris with Bahama Negro Dancers; *Dance of Exuberance* Tamiris; *Dirge* Tamiris *Maenad* Tamiris; [*Congo* Bahama Negro Dancers]; *South American Dance* Tamiris; *Impressions of the Bull Ring* Tamiris; [*The Jumpin' Dance* and *The Fire Dance* Bahama Negro Dancers]

Orchestral Conductor, Hans Lange; Tamiris costumes, Tamiris

Radio City Music Hall Appearance

Tamiris, "Noted Exponent of the Modern Dance"

Aug 24–30 1933   New York: Radio City Music Hall

[The Radio City Symphony Orchestra with featured guests, the Corps de Ballet and The Roxyettes; Sigmund Spaeth]; *South American Dance* Tamiris; *Impressions of the Bull Ring* Tamiris; [The Roxyettes; Music Hall News; *A Bit O' Old Ireland* with guests and the Corps de Ballet; Movie, *Paddy, The Next Best Thing* with Janet Gaynor and Warner Baxter; Music Hall Grand Organ]

3 Tamiris and Her Group, 1934–1936

THE MATURE ARTISTIC entity which came to be known as Tamiris and her Group made its first major appearance on January 14 1934 with a cycle of dances entitled *Walt Whitman Suite*. From then until the production of the dramatic *Momentum* on November 8 1936 Tamiris was a force in the modern dance equal to any of the others who were also shaping its form: Martha Graham, Doris Humphrey, Hanya Holm, Charles Weidman, Louis Horst, John Martin, Martha Hill. Tamiris participated in its development, gave it its substance, kept it "modern," i.e., aware of its time. She helped determine, and ever confirmed, its name.

Social protest was the stimulus which impinged most upon the consciousness of a Tamiris during this period and caused dynamic group works of head-on power: *Six Negro Spirituals*, a moving combination of pathos and joy; *Walt Whitman Suite*, a vital statement of yearning and being; *Toward the Light*, a preoccupation with freedom and existence; *Group Dance*, a sarcastic deriding of effeminacy and decadence; *Cycle of Unrest*, a writhing manifesto of conflict and optimism; *Harvest 1935*, a revolting denunciation of war; *Momentum*, a dramatic encounter between "haves" and "have-nots."

The concert dance called *Mass Study* and the theatre dances in the play *Gold Eagle Guy* were two results of her Group Theatre affiliation which developed into a reciprocal arrangement whereby Tamiris taught movement classes to its actors and it gave acting classes to her dancers. Lee Strasberg's adaptation of the Stanislavsky method was an important affirmation and clarification for Tamiris of her own approach to theatrical performance, direction, and choreography. It confirmed her search for the specific human motivation for movement, rather than the reach for the abstract artistic application. Later development would see her more at home in the theatre enterprise that spoke to the many than in the concert hall cult that appealed to the few.

Tamiris never belonged to any exclusive set, although she instigated and supported many projects. She just was Tamiris. The big four of Graham-Holm-Humphrey-Weidman, together with Horst and Hill, made up the Bennington group.[23] Tamiris was too much of a maverick to be happy in a rarified college atmosphere or satisfied with the esoteric artistic stratosphere which these artists inhabited. Nor did

---

[23] At Bennington College in Vermont, between 1934 and 1941 (summer 1939 at Mills College), workshops (organized by Martha Hill and Mary Jo Shelly) featured artists Graham, Holm, Humphrey, and Weidman to teach classes, repertory, and theatre technique. Horst and Arch Lauterer were also staff members.

she belong to the revolutionary dancers like Anna Sokolow who were submerged in protest and propaganda. Tamiris believed too much in the power of the individual to let herself be lost among or be used by the proletarian masses. At the same time, though she was never included in either group, she belonged to both. She was just as much devoted to "art" as the ascetic Graham or the intellectual Humphrey; she was just as much immersed in the problems of the day as the mercurial Sokolow. The belonging and the not-belonging made for a dichotomy of acceptance-non-acceptance that would have worn down a lesser human being. Despite constant adverse criticism, Tamiris just went on being Tamiris, facing the dynamic actuality of the world with her un-selfconscious optimism.

Everyone admitted that she could dance gloriously; all as readily agreed that she did not know how to choreograph, i.e., could not make a dance according to the Horst code.[24] It was all right for Humphrey to follow the symphonic form; Graham could use stream of consciousness with climactic orgasm; Weidman could use pantomime with dramatic flare; but Tamiris could not make artistic statements that used social themes so obviously. Her dances did not develop enough, or they were too repetitious, or they were too literal, or her symbols stayed too much on the sensory and superficial level. She never achieved "significant form"; she failed to discipline her material. So said the mouthpiece of the new estheticians, *The Dance Observer*.

On the other hand, for the revolutionary dancers, she could not propagandize, i.e. could not give a message according to the rules of their movement. Her dances were too illusory, or they did not move her audience, or they were too bourgeois, or her themes dwelt too consistently on the decadent (i.e., "abstract") plane. She never achieved didactic statement; she failed to clarify her material. So said the mouthpiece of the propaganda-mongers, the *Daily Worker*.

Caught between two opposing camps, group works produced by Tamiris during these three years never had a chance to be accepted. She was neither a Graham nor a Sokolow. Her *Walt Whitman Suite* which combined Whitman and jazz had no climax; its lyricism which flowed without peaks was old-fashioned as was its optimistic message. *Toward the Light* which depicted revolution was too obvious; its bold use of numbers (*No 1, No 2,* etc.) instead of sub-titles was considered pointless since the progression from oppression to massing to revolt to freedom could be understood. *Cycle of Unrest* which stated universal conflicts was confusing; its optimistic affirmation of the individual enriched by the mass was misunderstood as merely following the popular formula of revolt. *Harvest 1935* which satirized opportunism and war was tawdry; its forthright use of burlesque was deemed too lusty and low for the concert stage. *Momentum* which followed a dramatic sequence was—dramatic; its conflict between the "haves" and the "have-nots" was too logical for abstract theatre dance.

[24] See his book *Pre-Classic Dance Forms* (New York: Kamin Dance Publishers 1953). Beginning in 1928, Louis Horst taught for years a composition course which contained the implied code for criticism printed in his magazine *The Dance Observer*.

In short, Tamiris was damned if she did and damned if she didn't, by one camp or the other. But the non-climactic flow of Tamiris choreography was perfect to express the breadth of Whitman. The use of numbers for titles of the parts of *Toward the Light* was vital in depicting the clicking off of the inevitable process of revolution. On the other hand, the provocative sub-titles of *Cycle of Unrest* mirrored the disruption of her period: *Protest, The Individual and the Mass, Affirmation, Camaraderie,* and *Conflict,* especially when expressed with the Tamiris drive—simple, direct, and strenuous. Tamiris was never afraid to use burlesque if her material required it: How better to depict the war she ridiculed in the part of *Harvest 1935* called *Manoeuvres?* Bad taste to have human projectiles erupt from a human cannon? No worse than the phenomenon it satirized. And the dramatic *Momentum,* in which Tamiris as a night club danseuse stole the show, needed the blast of naïveté of such an episode to expose the inhumanity of the preceding section's murdering nightriders.

Driven to the reactions her time required, Tamiris pleased few, but no one could deny that she was a major force in the a-borning modern dance. She faced her reality and tried to inaugurate an esthetic out of the stimuli that hit her. Not very many liked either what she had to say or how she said it, but no one could deny her sincerity or passion.

Nor her effect. As she was left out of the Bennington group because she might teach bad choreography by practice, so she was never in the revolutionary dancers because she might teach abstract principles by example. Neither wanted her in their camp—unless she changed, an impossibility—but neither could they ignore her since she went on being what she was: Tamiris, the dancer who moved with the body electric through the halcyon days of her here and now, the American 1930s.

Premiere of Walt Whitman Suite

Tamiris and her Group

Jan 14 1934   eve   New York: Booth Theatre

Mirage Tamiris; *Hypocrisy* Tamiris; *Walt Whitman Suite: Salut au Monde* "You, whoever you are . . ." (Tamiris / Pitot) Tamiris, *Song of the Open Road* 1st mvmt "These yearnings, why are they . . ." (Tamiris / Pitot) Sydne Becker, Hilda Sheldon, Dvo Seron, Ida Soyer and Ida Tarvin, *I Sing the Body Electric* ("The female contains all qualities and tempers them, She is in her place and moves with perfect balance, She is all things duly veiled, She is both passive and active . . .") (Tamiris / Pitot) Tamiris, *Song of the Open Road* 2nd mvmt ("My call is the call of battle . . .") (Tamiris / Pitot) Sydne Becker, Ida Soyer and Ida Tarvin, *Halcyon Days* ("The brooding and blissful halcyon days!") (Tamiris / Pitot) Tamiris, *Song of the Open Road* 3rd mvmt ("Afoot and light hearted I take to the open road. . . . Still here I carry my old delicious burdens . . .") (Tamiris / Pitot) Tamiris with Sydne Becker, Molly Bornn, Hilda Sheldon, Dvo Seron, Ida Soyer and Ida Tarvin; *Cymbal Dance* Ida Soyer and Ida Tarvin; *Maenad* Tamiris; *Composition for Group* Sydne Becker, Molly Bornn, Freda Granett, Hilda Sheldon, Dvo Seron, Ida Soyer, Ida Tarvin and Greta Wilde; *Three Negro Spirituals: Swing Low, Sweet Chariot, Git on Board*

Walt Whitman Suite Premiere, cont
Lil Chillen and *Go Down Moses* Tamiris; *Twentieth Century Bacchante* Tamiris; *Impressions of the Bull Ring* Tamiris

Piano, Genevieve Pitot; costumes, Tamiris

Students' Dance Recitals, Washington Irving High School

Tamiris and her Group

Mar 10 1934[25]   eve   New York: Municipal Auditorium

Mirage Tamiris; *Hypocrisy* Tamiris; *Walt Whitman Suite: Salut au Monde* Tamiris, *Song of the Open Road* 1st mvmt Sydne Becker, Hilda Sheldon, Dvo Seron, Ida Soyer and Ida Tarvin, *I Sing the Body Electric* Tamiris, *Song of the Open Road* 2nd mvmt Sydne Becker, Ida Soyer and Ida Tarvin, *Halcyon Days* Tamiris, *Song of the Open Road* 3rd mvmt Tamiris with Sydne Becker, Molly Bornn, Hilda Sheldon, Dvo Seron, Ida Soyer and Ida Tarvin; *Cymbal Dance* Ida Soyer and Ida Tarvin; *Maenad* Tamiris; *Composition for Group* Sydne Becker, Molly Bornn, Freda Granett, Hilda Sheldon, Dvo Seron, Ida Soyer, Ida Tarvin and Greta Wilde; *Three Negro Spirituals: Swing Low, Sweet Chariot, Git on Board Lil Chillen* and *Go Down Moses* Tamiris; *Twentieth Century Bacchante* Tamiris; *Impressions of the Bull Ring* Tamiris

Piano, Genevieve Pitot; costumes, Tamiris

Premiere of Toward the Light

Tamiris and her Group

Apr 15 1934   mat   New York: Little Theatre

Maenad Tamiris; *Dirge* Tamiris; *Toward the Light: No 1* (Tamiris / Henry Brant) Tamiris, *No 2* (Tamiris / Henry Brant) Tamiris, *No 3* (Tamiris / Henry Brant, arr Genevieve Pitot) Sydne Becker, Dvo Seron, Hilda Sheldon, Ida Soyer and Ida Tarvin, *No 4* (Tamiris / Henry Brant) Tamiris, *No 5* (Tamiris / Henry Brant, arr Genevieve Pitot) Ruth Baker, Sydne Becker, Molly Bornn, Helen Cross, Freda Granett, Nina Hartman, Fay Marsh, Dvo Seron, Hilda Sheldon, Isabel Simons, Ida Soyer, Ida Tarvin, Ray White and Greta Wilde; *Walt Whitman Suite: Salut au Monde* Tamiris, *Song of the Open Road* 1st mvmt Sydne Becker, Hilda Sheldon, Dvo Seron, Ida Soyer and Ida Tarvin, *I Sing the Body Electric* Tamiris, *Song of the Open Road* 2nd mvmt Sydne Becker, Ida Soyer and Ida Tarvin, *Halcyon Days* Tamiris, *Song of the Open Road* 3rd mvmt Tamiris with Sydne Becker, Molly Bornn, Hilda Sheldon, Dvo Seron, Ida Soyer and Ida Tarvin; *Twentieth Century Bacchante* Tamiris; *Composition for Group* Sydne Becker, Molly Bornn, Freda Granett, Hilda Sheldon, Dvo Seron, Ida Soyer, Ida Tarvin and Greta Wilde; *South American Dance* Tamiris

Piano, Genevieve Pitot and Mercedes Bennett; costumes, Tamiris

Premiere of Group Dance

Tamiris and her Group   New Masses Benefit

May 27 1934   eve   New York: City College Auditorium

Salut au Monde Tamiris; *Song of the Open Road* 2nd mvmt Sydne Becker, Ida Soyer and Ida Tarvin; *Hypocrisy* Tamiris; *Dirge* Tamiris; *Composition for Group* Sydne Becker, Molly Bornn, Freda Granett, Hilda Sheldon, Dvo Seron, Ida Soyer and Ida

---

[25] There is evidence that Tamiris and her Group appeared on Jan 28 1934 at the 44th Street Theatre at a Benefit for the American Committee for the Relief of German Children; no program is available.

Tamiris and Her Group, 1934-1936

Tarvin; *Toward the Light: No 1* Tamiris, *No 2* Tamiris, *No 3* Sydne Becker, Dvo Seron, Hilda Sheldon, Ida Soyer and Ida Tarvin, *No 4* Tamiris, *No 5* Ruth Baker, Sydne Becker, Molly Bornn, Helen Cross, Freda Granett, Nina Hartman, Fay Leejia, Dvo Seron, Hilda Sheldon, Isabel Simons, Ida Soyer, Ida Tarvin and Ray White; *Dance for a Holiday* Sydne Becker, Dvo Seron, Hilda Sheldon, Ida Soyer and Ida Tarvin; *South American Dance* Tamiris; *Group Dance* (Tamiris / Henry Brant) Ruth Baker, Sydne Becker, Molly Bornn, Helen Cross, Freda Granett, Nina Hartman, Fay Leejia, Ruth Nelson, Dorothy Patten, Sophie Salpeter, Dvo Seron, Hilda Sheldon, Isabel Simons, Ida Soyer, Ida Tarvin and Ray White; *Negro Spirituals: Nobody Knows de Trouble I See, Swing Low, Sweet Chariot, Git on Board Lil Chillen, Go Down Moses* and *Joshua Fit de Battle ob Jericho* Tamiris; *Twentieth Century Bacchante* Tamiris

Piano, Genevieve Pitot and Mercedes Bennett; costumes, Tamiris

Gold Eagle Guy

History: Opened Nov 28 1934 New York: Morosco Theatre Moved Dec 25 1934 to Belasco Theatre Closed after 66 performances

Production details: Production, The Group Theatre, Inc, in association with D. A. Doran, Jr; book, Melvin Levy; direction, Lee Strasberg; settings, Donald Oenslager; costumes, Kay Morrison; dances, Tamiris

Cast: Phoebe Brand, Helen Carrm, Paula Miller, Ruth Nelson, Eunice Stoddard and Florence Cooper as Dancing Girls, Evelyn Geller, Joan Madison and Dorothy Patten as Other Girls, Frances Williams as Mrs Kummer, Roman Bohnen as Macondray, Gerrit Kraber as Tony Sorrenson, Walter Coy as Adam Keane, J. Edward Bromberg as Guy Button, Herbert Ratner as Bartender, Bob Lewis as Gus a Waiter, Jack Kaiser as Accordion Ed, Clifford Odets as Burns, Morris Carnovsky as Will Parrott, Sanford Meisner as Ortega, Luther Adler as Emperor Norton, William Challee as Pearly, Art Smith as Merg, Elia Kazan as Polyzoides, Jules Garfield as Sailor, Stella Adler as Adah Menken, Alan Baxter as MacNaurty, Lewis Leverett as A Miner, David Kortchmar as Another Miner, Russell Collins as A Deserter, Lewis Leverett as Captain Roberts, Russell Collins as Ed Walker, Margaret Barker as Jessie Sargent, Luther Adler as Tang Sin, Clifford Odets as Jolais, Gerrit Kraber as Joe, Jules Garfield as Mackay, Phoebe Brand as Elizabeth Jolais, Florence Cooper as Mrs DaSilva, Joan Madison as Mrs Muller, Dorothy Patten as Miss Simmonds, Marietta Bitter as Miss Crackle a harpist, Paula Miller as Mrs Sheldon, Lewis Leverett as Andre, William Challee as Ah Kee, Eunice Stoddard as Mrs Lemon, Frances Williams as Mrs Guadalla, Herbert Ratner as Jacobs, Art Smith as Wallin, Alan Baxter as Kohler, Alexander Kirkland as Lon Firth, Helen Carrm as Mrs Halstead, Ruth Nelson as Mrs McElvay, Jackie Jordan as Guy Jr, David Kortchmar as Rev Brown, Alan Baxter as Postman, Sanford Meisner as Guy Jr (Act 3), Bob Lewis as Okajima, Herbert Ratner as A D. T. Boy, Paula Miller as Mrs Nass and Ruth Nelson as Miss Richards

Scenes: I, The Mantic Barroom, San Francisco, 1862; II, Offices of the Keane Shipping Company, San Francisco, 1864; III, Parlor of Guy Button's California Street Home, San Francisco, 1879; IV, Same as II, but now the offices of the Gold Eagle Lines, March, 1898; V, Guy Button's private offices in the home office of the Gold Eagle Lines, San Francisco, early on the morning of April 18th 1906

Premiere of *Cycle of Unrest*

Tamiris and her Group

Jan 13 1935 eve New York: Civic Repertory Theatre Presented by The Theatre Union

Walt Whitman Suite: Halcyon Days Tamiris, *Song of the Open Road* 1st mvmt Sydne Becker, Hilda Sheldon, Dvo Seron, Ida Soyer and Ida Tarvin, *I Sing the Body*

Cycle of Unrest Premiere, cont
Electric Tamiris; *Cycle of Unrest: Protest* (Tamiris / E. Seigmeister) Tamiris; *The Individual and the Mass* (Tamiris / P. Hindemith) Tamiris with Sydne Becker, Molly Bornn, Freda Granett, Hilda Sheldon, Dvo Seron, Ida Soyer and Ida Tarvin, *Affirmation* (Tamiris / A. Mossolow) Tamiris, *Camaraderie* (Tamiris / E. Seigmeister) Sydne Becker, Hilda Sheldon, Ida Soyer and Ida Tarvin, *Conflict* (Tamiris / Henry Brant) Ida Abel, Ruth Baker, Sydne Becker, Molly Bornn, Prudence Bredt, Freda Granett, Fay Leejia, Ruth Nelson, Dorothy Patten, Gertrude Peyser, Sophie Salpeter, Dvo Seron, Hilda Sheldon, Ida Soyer, Ida Tarvin and Ray White; *Toward the Light: No 1 (Freedom)* Tamiris and *No 5 (Work and Play)* Ruth Baker, Sydne Becker, Molly Bornn, Prudence Bredt, Freda Granett, Fay Leejia, Gertrude Peyser, Sophie Salpeter, Dvo Seron, Hilda Sheldon, Ida Soyer, Ida Tarvin and Ray White; *Dirge* Tamiris; *Hypocrisy* Tamiris; *Twentieth Century Bacchante* Tamiris

Piano, Genevieve Pitot

Dance League Program

Red Dancers, New Dance Group, The Dance Unit and Tamiris Group

Feb 17 1935   New York: Center Theatre   Presented by Major Revolutionary Workers Dance League in conjunction with National Theatre Week

[*Black and White* (Edith Segal, director /   ) Red Dancers Irving Lansky and Ad Bates; *Themes from a Slavic People* (/ Bartok) Sophie Maslow; *Van der Lubbe's Head* (/ Poem, Alfred Hayes) New Dance Group; *Diplomacy and War* and *Protest* from *The Anti-War Cycle* (/ North) The Dance Unit; *Defiance* (/ Honegger) Lily Mehlman]; *Conflict* from *Cycle of Unrest* Tamiris Group; [*Charity* (/ arr Parnas) New Dance Group; *Parasite* from a group of *Three Poster Dances* (/ Heller) Nadia Chilkovsky; *Woman* from *The Disinherited* (/ Parnas) Miriam Blecher; *Histrionics* (/ Hindemith) Anna Sokolow; *Forces in Opposition* (/ Swift) The Dance Unit; *Time is Money* (/ Poem, S. Furnaroff) Jane Dudley]; *Work and Play* [*No 5*] from *Toward the Light* Tamiris Group

Piano for Tamiris, Genevieve Pitot

Students' Dance Recitals, Washington Irving High School

Tamiris and her Group

Mar 8 1935   eve   New York: Municipal Auditorium

Walt Whitman Suite: Halcyon Days Tamiris, *Song of the Open Road* 1st mvmt Sydne Becker, Hilda Sheldon, Dvo Seron, Ida Soyer and Ida Tarvin; *I Sing the Body Electric* Tamiris; *Cycle of Unrest: Protest* Tamiris, *The Individual and the Mass* Tamiris with Sydne Becker, Molly Bornn, Freda Granett, Hilda Sheldon, Dvo Seron, Ida Soyer and Ida Tarvin, *Affirmation* Tamiris, *Camaraderie* Sydne Becker, Hilda Sheldon, Ida Soyer and Ida Tarvin; *Conflict* Ida Abel, Ruth Baker, Sydne Becker, Molly Bornn, Prudence Bredt, Freda Granett, Fay Leejia, Ruth Nelson, Dorothy Patten, Gertrude Peyser, Sophie Salpeter, Dvo Seron, Hilda Sheldon, Ida Soyer, Ida Tarvin and Ray White; *Toward the Light: No 1 (Freedom)* Tamiris, *No 2 (Dance of War)* Tamiris and *No 5 (Work and Play)* Ruth Baker, Sydne Becker, Molly Bornn, Prudence Bredt, Freda Granett, Fay Leejia, Gertrude Peyser, Sophie Salpeter, Dvo Seron, Hilda Sheldon, Ida Soyer, Ida Tarvin and Ray White; *Dirge* Tamiris; *Twentieth Century Bacchante* Tamiris

Piano, Genevieve Pitot

I   Tamiris in *The Queen Walks in the Garden*, 1927 (Photograph by Soichi Sunami)
Dance Collection

II Tamiris and Her Group in (a) Triangle Dance, 1931 (Photograph by Soichi Sunami), and (b) *How Long, Brethren,* 1937 (WPA Federal Theatre Photograph)
Dance Collection

III Tamiris in *Go Down, Moses*, 1933 *Dance Collection*

IV Tamiris in two dances from the *Walt Whitman Suite,* circa January 1934: (a) Halcyon Days, and (b) *Salut au Monde* (Photograph by Thomas Bouchard)
Dance Collection

V (a) *Wild Horse Ceremonial Dance* with Daniel Nagrin and company, 1946, from *Annie Get Your Gun,* choreography by Tamiris (Photograph by Vandamm Studio); (b) *Currier and Ives* number, 1947, from *Up in Central Park,* choreography by Tamiris (Photograph by Universal Pictures Co., Inc.   *Dance Collection*

VI Tamiris, in the early 1950s *Dance Collection*

Tamiris and Her Group, 1934-1936

Premiere of Mass Study

Tamiris and her Group

Mar 31 1935   New York: Civic Repertory Theatre

Mirage Tamiris; *Cycle of Unrest: Protest* Tamiris, *Individual and The Mass* Tamiris with Sydne Becker, Molly Bornn, Freda Granett, Hilda Sheldon, Dvo Seron, Ida Soyer and Ida Tarvin, *Camaraderie* Sydne Becker, Hilda Sheldon, Ida Soyer and Ida Tarvin, *Affirmation* Tamiris and *Conflict* Ida Able, Ruth Baker, Sydne Becker, Molly Bornn, Prudence Bredt, Freda Granett, Fay Leejia, Ruth Nelson, Dorothy Patten, Gertrude Peyser, Sophie Salpeter, Dvo Seron, Hilda Sheldon, Ida Soyer, Ida Tarvin and Ray White; *Dance of Escape* (Tamiris / E. Seigmeister) Tamiris; *Flight* (Tamiris / A. Mossolow) Tamiris; *Mass Study* (Tamiris / Bartok) Ruth Baker, Sydne Becker, Molly Bornn, Prudence Bredt, Robert Dublirer, Freda Granett, Judith Gross, Sydne Hoffman, Elia Kazan, Gerrit Kraber, Lewis Leverett, Paula Miller, Ruth Nelson, Gertrude Peyser, Sophie Salpeter, Maurice Silvers, Dvo Seron, Hilda Sheldon, Ida Soyer and Ida Tarvin; *Toward the Light: No 3 (Elements)* Sydne Becker, Hilda Sheldon, Dvo Seron, Ida Soyer, Ida Tarvin and Ray White, *No 4 (War)* Tamiris and *No 5 (Work and Play)* Ruth Baker, Sydne Becker, Molly Bornn, Prudence Bredt, Freda Granett, Fay Leejia, Gertrude Peyser, Sophie Salpeter, Dvo Seron, Hilda Sheldon, Ida Soyer, Ida Tarvin and Ray White; *Dirge* Tamiris; *Composition for Group* Ida Abel, Sydne Becker, Molly Bornn, Freda Granett, Dvo Seron, Hilda Sheldon, Ida Soyer and Ida Tarvin; *Three Negro Spirituals: Swing Low, Sweet Chariot, Go Down Moses* and *Joshua Fit de Battle ob Jericho* Tamiris

Piano, Genevieve Pitot and Mercedes Bennett

June Dance Festival Program

Dance Unit, Tamiris Group, Ruth Allerhand Group, New Dance Group and Charles Weidman Group

June 9 1935   eve   New York: Park Theatre   Presented by New Dance League

[*Pioneer Marches* (/ Prokofieff) Dance Unit]; *Camaraderie* from *Cycle of Unrest* Tamiris Group; *Escape* Tamiris; *Individual and the Mass* from *Cycle of Unrest* Tamiris with group; *Flight* Tamiris; *Work and Play* [*No 5*] from *Toward the Light* Tamiris Group; [*Strange American Funeral* (Sokolow / Seigmeister) Dance Unit; *Winning Group of Afternoon Performance* (?); *Strike* (/ McDowell) Ruth Allerhand and group; *Ah Peace* (/ Kodaly) New Dance Group; *Traditions* (Weidman / Engel) Charles Weidman, Jose Limon and Bill Matons; *We Remember* (/ Parnas) New Dance Group; *Studies in Conflict* (Weidman / Rudyhar) Charles Weidman, Jose Limon and group]

Dancers in Tamiris Group: Ruth Baker, Sydne Becker, Molly Bornn, Prudence Bredt, Freda Granett, Fay Leejia, Gertrude Peyser, Sophie Salpeter, Hilda Sheldon, Dvo Seron, Ida Soyer, Ida Tarvin and Ray White

Piano for Tamiris, Genevieve Pitot

Premiere of Harvest 1935

Tamiris and her Group

Nov 11 1935   eve   New York: Venice Theatre   Sponsored by New Dance League and *New Theatre Magazine*

Affirmation from *Cycle of Unrest* Tamiris; *Song of the Open Road* 1st mvmt from   *Walt Whitman Suite* Sydne Becker, Hilda Sheldon, Dvo Seron, Ida Soyer and Ida

Harvest 1935 Premiere, cont
Tarvin; *Dance of War* from *Towards the Light* Tamiris; *Dance of Escape* Tamiris; *Harvest 1935: Sycophants* (Tamiris / Hindemith) Tamiris with Sydne Becker, Molly Bornn, Dvo Seron, Ida Soyer and Ida Tarvin, *Middle Ground* (Tamiris / Shostakovitch) Tamiris and *Manoeuvres* (Tamiris / Hindemith-Debussy) Tamiris with Ida Abel, Ruth Baker, Sydne Becker, Molly Bornn, Sydne Hoffman, Gertrude Peyser, Sophie Salpeter, Dvo Seron, Hilda Sheldon, Ida Soyer, Ida Tarvin and Ray White; *Camaraderie* Sydne Becker, Hilda Sheldon, **Ida** Soyer and Ida Tarvin; *Dirge* Tamiris; *Flight* Tamiris; *Individual and the Mass* from *Cycle of Unrest* Tamiris with Sydne Becker, Molly Bornn, Hilda Sheldon, Dvo Seron, Ida Soyer and Ida Tarvin; *Mass Study* Ida Abel, Ruth Baker, Sydne Becker, Molly Bornn, Sydne Hoffman, Gertrude Peyser, Sophie Salpeter, Dvo Seron, Hilda Sheldon, Ida Soyer, Ida Tarvin and Ray White

Piano, Genevieve Pitot; tympani, S. Gershek; flute, A. del Vecchio

Carnegie Hall Modern Dancers Program

Martha Graham, Doris Humphrey & Charles Weidman, Tamiris, Dance Unit

Dec 15 1935 eve   New York: Carnegie Hall   Presented by Committee on Cultural Activities, International Labor Defense

Part I
Martha Graham and Dance Group[26]

Part II
Harvest 1935: Sycophants Tamiris with Sydne Becker, Molly Bornn, Dvo Seron, Ida Soyer and Ida Tarvin, *Middle Ground* Tamiris and *Manoeuvres* Tamiris with Ida Abel, Ruth Baker, Sydne Becker, Molly Bornn, Sydne Hoffman, Gertrude Peyser, Hilda Sheldon, Sophie Salpeter, Dvo Seron, Ida Soyer, Ida Tarvin and Ray White; *Work and Play* from *Toward the Light* Ida Abel, Ruth Baker, Sydne Becker, Molly Bornn, Sydne Hoffman, Gertrude Peyser, Sophie Salpeter, Hilda Sheldon, Dvo Seron, Ida Soyer, Ida Tarvin and Ray White

Piano, Genevieve Pitot; flute, A. del Vecchio; tympani, S. Gershek

Part III
Doris Humphrey, Charles Weidman **and** Groups[27]

Part IV
Dance Unit of New Dance League, Anna Sokolow, Director[28]

---

[26] *Celebration* (Graham / Louis Horst) group; *Imperial Gesture* (Graham / Lehman Engel) Graham; *Course* (Graham / George Antheil) group
   Group members: Anita Alverez, Bonnie Bird, Dorothy Bird, Ethel Butler, Lil Liandre, Marie Marchowsky, Sophie Maslow, Lily Mehlman, May O'Donnell, Florence Schneider, Kathleen Slagle, Gertrude Shurr and Anna Sokolow

[27] *New Dance: Prelude, Processional, Celebration* and *Variations and Conclusion* (Humphrey / Wallingford Riegger) Humphrey, Weidman and group; *Stock Exchange* from *Atavisms* (Weidman / Lehman Engel) Weidman and group
   Group members for *New Dance*: Letitia Ide, Katherine Manning, Ada Korvin, Katharine Litz, Beatrice Seckler, Joan Levy, Sybil Shearer, Edith Orcutt, Mariam Krakovsky, Jose Limon, Kenneth Bostock and George Bockman
   Group members for *Stock Exchange*: Jose Limon, Bill Matons, Kenneth Bostock, George Bockman, Morris Bakst, Jerry Davidson, Maurice Zilbert, Lee Sherman, Harry Cable, William Bales, Ezra Friedman, Gene Oliver and Joseph Belsky

[28] *Strange American Funeral* (Sokolow / Poem, Michael Gold and music, Seigmeister) Dance Unit group
   Group: Asa Cefkin, Ronya Chermin, Celia Dembroe, Ruth Freedman, Eleanor Lapidus, Rose Levy, Marie Marchowsky, Ruth Nisenson and Florence Schneider

Tamiris and Her Group, 1934-1936

Students' Dance Recitals, Washington Irving High School

Tamiris and her Group

Jan 11 1936 eve New York: Municipal Auditorium

Camaraderie from *Cycle of Unrest* Sydne Becker, Hilda Sheldon, Ida Soyer and Ida Tarvin; *Dance of War* [No 2] from *Toward the Light* Tamiris; *Escape* Tamiris; *Harvest 1935: Sycophants* Tamiris with Sydne Becker, Hilda Sheldon, Dvo Seron, Ida Soyer and Ida Tarvin, *Middle Ground* Tamiris and *Manouevers* Tamiris with Ada Abel, Ruth Baker, Sydne Becker, Sydne Hoffman, Gertrude Peyser, Sophie Salpeter, Hilda Sheldon, Dvo Seron, Ida Soyer, Ida Tarvin and Ray White; *Conflict* from *Cycle of Unrest* Ada Abel, Ruth Baker, Sydne Becker, Gertrude Peyser, Sophie Salpeter, Hilda Sheldon, Dvo Seron, Ida Soyer, Ida Tarvin and Ray White; *Flight* Tamiris; *Dirge* Tamiris; *Song of the Open Road* 1st mvmt from *Walt Whitman Suite* Sydne Becker, Hilda Sheldon, Dvo Seron, Ida Soyer and Ida Tarvin; *Three Negro Spirituals: Go Down Moses, Git on Board Lil Chillen, Joshua Fit de Battle ob Jericho* Tamiris; *Mass Study* Ada Abel, Ruth Baker, Sydne Becker, Sydne Hoffman, Gertrude Peyser, Sophie Salpeter, Hilda Sheldon, Dvo Seron, Ida Soyer, Ida Tarvin and Ray White

Piano, Genevieve Pitot

Brooklyn Museum Dance Recital

Tamiris and her Group

Feb 8 1936 11 AM Brooklyn: Museum Sculpture Court

Camaraderie from *Cycle of Unrest* Sydne Becker, Hilda Sheldon, Ida Soyer and Ida Tarvin; *Flight* Tamiris; *Song of the Open Road* 1st mvmt from *Walt Whitman Suite* Sydne Becker, Hilda Sheldon, Dvo Seron, Ida Soyer and Ida Tarvin; *Work and Play* from *Toward the Light* Ada Abel, Sydne Becker, Ruth Baker, Gertrude Peyser, Dvo Seron, Sophie Salpeter, Hilda Sheldon, Ida Soyer, Ida Tarvin and Ray White; *Sycophants* from *Harvest 1935* Tamiris with Sydne Becker, Hilda Sheldon, Dvo Seron, Ida Soyer and Ida Tarvin; *Manoeuvres* from *Harvest 1935* Tamiris with Ada Abel, Sydne Becker, Ruth Baker, Sydne Hoffman, Gertrude Peyser, Dvo Seron, Sophie Salpeter, Hilda Sheldon, Ida Soyer, Ida Tarvin and Ray White; *Three Negro Spirituals: Go Down Moses, Git on Board Lil Chillen* and *Joshua Fit de Battle ob Jericho* Tamiris; *Impressions of the Bull Ring* Tamiris

Piano, Genevieve Pitot

Program for American League against War and Fascism

Tamiris and her Group

Mar 1 1936 Presented by Boro Park Branch

Protest from *Cycle of Unrest* Tamiris; *Song of the Open Road* 1st mvmt Nena Peters, Dvo Seron, Hilda Sheldon, Ida Soyer and Ida Tarvin; *Dance of Escape* Tamiris; *Composition for Group* Ada Abel, Nena Peters, Hilda Sheldon, Dvo Seron, Ida Soyer, Ida Tarvin and Ray White; *Harvest 1935: Sycophants* Tamiris with Nena Peters, Hilda Sheldon, Dvo Seron, Ida Soyer and Ida Tarvin, *Middle Ground* Tamiris and *Manoeuvres* Tamiris with Ada Abel, Ruth Baker, Sophie Salpeter, Gertrude Peyser, Nena Peters, Hilda Sheldon, Dvo Seron, Ida Soyer, Ida Tarvin and Ray White; *Song of the Open Road* 2nd mvmt Nena Peters, Ida Soyer and Ida Tarvin; *Flight* Tamiris; *Dance of War* from *Toward the Light* Tamiris; *Work and Play*

American League Program, cont
from *Toward the Light* Ada Abel, Ruth Baker, Sophie Salpeter, Gertrude Peyser, Nena Peters, Hilda Sheldon, Dvo Seron, Ida Soyer, Ida Tarvin and Ray White; *Four Negro Spirituals: Swing Low, Sweet Chariot, Go Down Moses, Git on Board Lil Chillen* and *Joshua Fit de Battle ob Jericho* Tamiris

Piano, Genevieve Pitot

YMHA Dance Concerts Series

Tamiris and her Group

Mar 8 1936   eve   New York: Kaufman Auditorium

Protest from *Cycle of Unrest* Tamiris; *Song of the Open Road* 1st mvmt from *Walt Whitman Suite* Nena Peters, Dvo Seron, Hilda Sheldon and Ida Soyer; *Dirge* Tamiris; *Dance of Escape* Tamiris; *Harvest 1935: Sycophants* Tamiris with Nena Peters, Hilda Sheldon, Dvo Seron and Ida Soyer, *Middle Ground* Tamiris and *Manoeuvres* Tamiris with Ada Abel, Ruth Baker, Sophie Salpeter, Gertrude Peyser, Nena Peters, Hilda Sheldon, Dvo Seron, Ida Soyer and Ray White; *Song of the Open Road* 2nd mvmt from *Walt Whitman Suite* Nena Peters, Ida Soyer and Dvo Seron; *Flight* Tamiris; *Dance of War* [*No 4*] from *Toward the Light* Tamiris; *Work and Play* [*No 5*] from *Toward the Light* Ada Abel, Ruth Baker, Sophie Salpeter, Gertrude Peyser, Nena Peters, Hilda Sheldon, Dvo Seron, Ida Soyer and Ray White; *Four Negro Spirituals: Swing Low, Sweet Chariot, Go Down Moses, Git on Board Lil Chillen* and *Joshua Fit de Battle ob Jericho* Tamiris

Piano, Genevieve Pitot

Midwest Tour Program

Tamiris and her Group

Presented by the Redpath Bureau[29]

Camaraderie from *Cycle of Unrest* Sydne Becker, Hilda Sheldon, Ida Soyer and Ida Tarvin; *Hypocrisy* Tamiris; *Song of the Open Road* 1st mvmt from *Walt Whitman Suite* Sydne Becker, Hilda Sheldon, Dvo Seron, Ida Soyer and Ida Tarvin; *Dirge* Tamiris; *Work and Play* [*No 5*] from *Toward the Light* Ada Abel, Sydne Becker, Molly Bornn, Hilda Sheldon, Dvo Seron, Ida Soyer and Ida Tarvin; *Negro Spirituals: Swing Low, Sweet Chariot, Git on Board Lil Chillen, Go Down Moses* and *Joshua Fit de Battle ob Jericho* Tamiris; *Dance for a Holiday* Sydne Becker, Dvo Seron, Hilda Sheldon, Ida Soyer and Ida Tarvin; *Impressions of the Bull Ring* Tamiris; *Composition for Group* Ada Abel, Sydne Becker, Molly Bornn, Dvo Seron, Hilda Sheldon, Ida Soyer and Ida Tarvin; *Twentieth Century Bacchante* Tamiris; *Manoeuvres* from *Harvest 1935* Tamiris with Ada Abel, Sydne Becker, Molly Bornn, Dvo Seron, Hilda Sheldon, Ida Soyer and Ida Tarvin

Piano, Genevieve Pitot

[29] On Dec 6 1935 Tamiris was in Chicago performing for the Union League Club, on Mar 26 1936 in LaCrosse, Wisconsin, at the Teachers College Auditorium. There is evidence that she also appeared at the University of Ohio in Bowling Green. However, details of other appearances on this tour are unavailable at this time. Of her experiences, she herself has written:
"The Red Path Bureau . . . booked me and a company of ten, through the Middle West in 1936. We danced in Wisconsin, Minnesota, Illinois, Iowa, Ohio, Indiana, Michigan. . . . As you can see, it was an extremely varied program from different periods of my career. The earlier dances were inevitably the best received by these audiences. On many of the university dates I combined the program, which generally took place in the evening, with a lecture-demonstration of technique during the day. An amusing sidelight on this tour was that most of the deans of the universities seemed to be so impressed with the fact that a dancer could also make sense when she spoke. They still connected the dance (of course they would never admit it) with

Premiere of Momentum

Tamiris and her Group

Nov 8 1936 eve   New York: Guild Theatre   Presented by New Dance League

Momentum: *Unemployed, SH!—SH!—, Legion, Nightriders, Diversion* and *Disclosure* (Tamiris / Herbert Haufreucht) Tamiris with group: Nucleus: Sydne Becker, Dvo Seron, Hilda Sheldon, Ida Soyer and Ida Tarvin and Apprentices: Ada Abel, Jilda Bronze, Rae Cohen, Vivian Cherry, Ann Goodson, Alma Lass, Gertrude Peyser, Florence Ross, Isabel Simon, Pearl Wall and Ray White; *Dance of Escape* Tamiris; *Composition for Group* Ada Abel, Sydne Becker, Ann Goodson, Hilda Sheldon, Dvo Seron, Ida Soyer, Ida Tarvin and Ray White; *Flight* Tamiris; Two Movements from *Harvest 1935*: *Middle Ground* Tamiris and *Manoeuvres* Tamiris with Ada Abel, Sydne Becker, Ann Goodson, Alma Lass, Gertrude Peyser, Florence Ross, Hilda Sheldon, Dvo Seron, Ida Soyer, Ida Tarvin, Pearl Wall and Ray White; *Impressions of the Bull Ring* Tamiris

Piano, Genevieve Pitot and Mercedes Bennett; clarinet, Louis Kline; trumpet, Louis Rubinstein; tympani, S. Gershek; costumes for *Momentum*, Resyl Krupnick and Stephanie Kline; masks for *Momentum*, Franziska Boas

---

the not-to-be-taken-too-seriously type of activity. In some sections it was truly pioneer work. In other places, where there had been some dance activity by Ted Shawn, the way was made a bit easier."

4 Tamiris and Her Sense of Mission, 1936–1939

DURING THE LATE DAYS of the month of December, 1936, the balletomane Lincoln Kirstein was made director of the New York Project of the Federal Dance Theatre, one of the five arts divisions of the Works Progress Administration.[30] The new director proposed to produce a spectacular revue that would depict a history of the dance.

"And I think you're the one to dance Isadora Duncan, Tamiris," he said to that staff choreographer who had been around the project since its inception in January of that year.

"And who will dance Tamiris?" the lady asked in return.

Within hours, Kirstein had returned to the ballet realm in which, despite its own problems of survival, order was assumed and authority was respected. Experience in the disordered, chaotic, and impudent world of that entity called Federal Dance Theatre cowed more than one supporter of dance, but its ever changing, always challenging, brutally alive and devastatingly frank characteristics made up the life-fulfilling world of a Tamiris. Dancers, who were people, were hungry; jobs, which were scarce, were fought for; reputations, which were at stake, were defended.

The story of this encounter points up two sides of the situation that was theatre dance in the Works Progress Administration. The modern choreographers, led by Tamiris, got dance into the Arts Project and, after it was in, made up its staff. Conversely, ballet dancers and ballet choreographers were mostly left out. Whether this was by deliberate action on the one side or conscious choice on the other, the scrappy moderns, used to the rough and tumble of hand-to-mouth existence since their art had begun just before the Depression, were right at home in the turmoil that was the center of the WPA Arts Project's very existence. Centuries old, ballet was foreign to the immediate "sense of mission" of the 1930s. Hilton Kramer, in an article entitled "The Nineteen-Thirties," uses the term "sense of mission" to describe the altruism "transcending the limits of individual careers" that "disparate groups enjoyed in the thirties" and "accounts for the vivid emotions still harbored for so difficult and desperate a period. Whatever the cause," he continued, "the emotions are real, and the passage of time has done little to dampen them."[31]

Fired by her sense of mission, Tamiris again was being Tamiris—reacting to the moment and its needs, responding to the now and its

---

[30] The other and older divisions were Theatre, Music, Art and Writing.
[31] *The New York Times Magazine* Oct 20 1968 p 23.

opportunities. In this, she, again, was the most modern of the modern dancers. Doris Humphrey and Charles Weidman were also staff choreographers, but neither gave up their individual careers for this mission of a public art as Tamiris did. She alone of all the major dancers working in the Thirties gave up her career, her group, almost her very self for the sense of purpose she felt in the Project. Her mission? To advance the welfare of the individuals who were dancers and, as importantly, to bring her art to a general public, not just to a narrow coterie.

As early as 1930 when she was organizing the Dance Repertory Theatre, which had plenty of difficulties although it was only a tiny organization of five artists, her group was labeled as one of the "Coxey's Army of the Concert World."[32] Undaunted, she served on the Board of Directors, with Agnes de Mille as president, of the Concert Dancers' League, organized to fight sabbath laws which were being used by the police to close dance concerts given on Sunday nights. Since this was the only night of the week when a theatre was available, the League was forced to advocate that concert dancers were like other concert artists—singers, pianists, violinists. These were allowed to appear on Sunday, while theatre activities, such as plays and musical comedies, were forbidden to play on the holy day. All the new modern dancers had to unite on this issue, because closure of theatres to them on Sunday meant no place at all to perform.

This was a specific issue, on which success was achieved, and the organization was soon allowed to founder like the Dance Repertory Theatre. But Tamiris saw greater goals for dancers united together for their own welfare: why should dancers not have a protective organization similar to the one that fellow theatre artists, the actors, had? They already had a union called Actors' Equity. By 1934, when the Depression had deepened and the plight of dancers had worsened, Tamiris proposed, at a meeting in her studio, a Dancers' Emergency Association with three aims: immediate cash relief for needy dancers, educational projects to provide jobs for dancers, and the control of dance studios. The last was specifically in protest to a proposed plan of the New York Board of Aldermen to license and regulate professional and trade schools. Cooperation was sought by other unions, whose representatives met at Tamiris' studio in May 1935, to decry that the Aldermen had chosen an already impoverished group as a source of revenue. Such licensing could result, the group declared, in the Board setting itself up as a censor of every form of cultural activity. The "Sullivan Bill" was defeated.

There were many social action groups in the thirties. One of the more militant was the Workers Dance League which changed its name to the New Dance League as the decade advanced. Often an affiliate but never a leader in the NDL, Tamiris appeared under its auspices at intervals—in concert or on forums. She also taught in its

---

[32] Sub-title, "A Study of the Ills and Ailments of the 'Serious' Dance Fields" *Dance Magazine* 15 (Dec 1930) 10, 52-53.

school which was formed by an alliance between it and the New Theatre League. The militancy of the two groups is most obvious in the avowed aims of its school: to give the student actor or director or theatre specialist of any kind a thorough technical training in his respective field and to convey to the student a clear understanding of the social functions of the theatre and dance of the time. There existed also a Dance Guild which served the needs of the young and apprentice artists. But Tamiris directed her manifold leadership abilities toward affiliating with the largest and most controversial of the institutions serving needy artists in the thirties, the Works Progress Administration. As soon as the Federal Theatre Project was formed in August 1935, under the direction of Hallie Flanagan, Tamiris took the lead and accomplished the feat of getting dancers as a group recognized for themselves rather than just as elements within the theatre part of the project. She did this by forming an organization called the Dance Association which she chaired. First by means of a Committee of 15 and then by a meeting of over one hundred dancers, Tamiris, through the resultant association, convinced Flanagan that a Dance Project should be set up. It began in January 1936.

The director of the Dance Project became Don Oscar Becque, not a big name on the stage or in the regular run of studio teaching. He had devoted himself to contemporary dance in its early stages, although his background was ballet. He happened to be the producer of one of two units already in operation under the Theatre Project and was moved to Director when the Dance Project was formed. He saw the main objectives of the new organization as, first, the development of a common denominator technique that would consider various movement demands of all types and varieties of dance requirements and, secondly, the extension of the boundaries of the American dance as to form and subject matter into full-length theatre pieces. So he wrote in *Federal Theatre Bulletin* 1 No 5, April 1936. Putting his two objectives into practice was another matter. The first was fought bitterly; the second was achieved successfully only by Tamiris.

The New York Dance Project had an executive committee consisting of Doris Humphrey, Tamiris, Felicia Sorel, Gluck-Sandor, and Charles Weidman. Donald Pond was named musical director, with assistants Genevieve Pitot and Wallingford Riegger. Given $155,000 to mount eight productions in six months, they all went to work—Becque on *Young Tramps,* Gluck-Sandor on *The Prodigal Son,* Sorel on *Til Eulenspiegel,* Humphrey on a re-staging of her *Suite in F,* Weidman on a new version of his dance based on *Candide,* and Tamiris on *Salut au Monde,* an extension of her *Walt Whitman Suite.* It was hoped that the first production would be put on the boards by the end of February.

Through the efforts of Grant Code at the Brooklyn Museum, the Majestic Theatre in Brooklyn was made available for the first production, a series of three matinees June 23, 24, 25, 1936 (Weidman's *Candide* and Humphrey's three dances, *Prelude* and *Celebration* with music by Roussel and *Parade* with music by Tcherepnine), although long before June, everyone realized that the aims set had been impossible to accomplish. When new appropriations were made July 1 1936, the Dance Project continued but with great difficulty. Red tape, bureaucratic reporting, personnel changing, budget inadequacies—all contributed to making chaotic the conditions under which a choreographer had to work. Nonetheless, Tamiris produced her *Salut au Monde* on August 5, also at the Majestic in Brooklyn.

Besides being a staff choreographer of the New York Project, Tamiris was continuing as chairman of the Dance Association which had been instrumental in the Project's formation. Joining with the New Dance League, the Dance Association sponsored a Dance Congress in May at the YMHA in New York. Ostensibly to be a Congress for the nation, it turned out, since it was hastily planned, to be a meeting of New York dancers who met, saw each other dance, and, as John Martin wrote bitterly, talked themselves to death. Already there was criticism of the administration of the Federal Dance Project, unhappiness which erupted in a Public Hearing on the Federal Dance Theatre in November. All attacked the Director, Becque, for not cutting through the red tape administratively and allowing productions to be put into theatres. Becque's *Young Tramps* again had to appear in Brooklyn after, like Gluck-Sandor's *The Eternal Prodigal*, it had been in rehearsal so long the dancers themselves were rebelling. Tamiris was one of those who led the attack on Becque, said he would not work with his choreographers, would not even meet with them. During the whole year there had been only three productions and a total of ten performances. And even closer to a choreographer's vanity was the fact that Becque was trying to enforce a common technique on all dancers—after some of the artists had spent their lives perfecting their own techniques, it was exclaimed. Such high-handedness was not to be tolerated. The session was a stormy one, with no one, not even the unfortunate Becque himself, there in defense.

He resigned in December 1936, after which followed the short directorship of Lincoln Kirstein and his abortive history of dance revue. No other director was appointed for dance, Stephen Karnot of the New York Theatre Project being named nominal head.

Tamiris was busy as well outside the Federal Dance Project as she continued to chair the Dance Association. Although a second more representative Dance Congress had been planned, no one took the lead sufficiently to pull it off; Tamiris soon had something else in mind. Working with friends in the New Dance League and the Dance Guild, she as chairman of the DA proposed an amalgamation of the three groups in order to eliminate overlapping functions and augment their power. Accordingly, the American Dance Association was organized at a conference in May 1937. Its constitution provided for two major sections of membership: the professional dancer and the non-professional (such as a student or an audience member). Separate committees would be formed to serve each group in the overall goal of helping dancers in their economic and artistic relationships. Tamiris, writing as president of the new organization, hoped the new set-up would widen the field of dance and clarify for the dancer himself his relationship to his work and his public. Specifically, the ADA hoped to safeguard the economic interests of dancers, to increase and equalize educational opportunities, and to promote the general welfare of the community through dance. The first evidence of the broad policy of the new group was the program on May 23 1937 given as a benefit for the aid of Spanish Democracy. Many kinds of dance—not just modern—were included. A mouthpiece, the *Herald*, was also launched.

During the same month Tamiris was steering this amalgamation, her major work for the Federal Dance Theatre was produced on Broadway. In a joint bill with Weidman's *Candide*,[33] her *How Long, Brethren?* opened on May 6 1937 and ran to standing-room-only houses for an unheard of forty-two performances. Its success gave the Federal Dance Project in New York respect both with audience and administration; ironically, it also gave Tamiris *Dance Magazine*'s first award for outstanding group choreography. The union of a great artist and a great theme constitutes, as Kierkegaard observed, "the fortunate in the historical process, the divine conjunction of its forces, the high tide of historic time." The conjunction of Tamiris the artist with her theme of the suffering Negro was the high tide of historic time for the Federal Dance Theatre. Never was such a conjunction more needed.

For the Federal Project was now being attacked by its own flank, the National Dance League, composed of the Dancing Masters of America, the English Folk Dancing Society of America, the Dancing Teachers Business Association of New York—i.e., the non-concert dancers. The main charge was that the entire dance project had been given over to "modernistic" dancing, which represented only one-twelfth of the dancers in New York. The dozen other types of dancing were ignored. Indeed, these "modernistic" dancers were not even professional dancers, for they danced on the side while they earned their support as clerks, stenographers, sales girls. Further resolutions made even more serious charges of "unparalleled unprofessionalism and shameful political agitation."

Political agitation such as picketing was deemed necessary as a means for change throughout the thirties. One of the more spectacular was the sit-in that occurred after one of the performances of the *How Long, Brethren?* and *Candide* bill. During the summer, the New York Project as well as all other Federal Theatre Projects had been staggered by the order to fire one-third of their personnel because of cut-backs by Congress. Led by Charles Weidman, the sit-in was in protest to this announced cut. Even part of the audience stayed on May 17 as the cast was joined by artists from other projects. The area around 44th Street became so jammed the police had to

---

[33] *Candide* was a condensed version of an earlier work for a full evening.

rope it off. The New York *Post* called it the first sit-in strike in the history of the American theatre.

Such political action did not prevent the cuts; the Federal Dance Project quietly merged again with the Theatre Project by October 1937. Ironically, theatre dance now had a spurt of activity it had never been able to achieve when it had more money. A Young Choreographers group which had been active sporadically during the early part of 1937 put on a Dance Program for Young Folks by Young Choreographers in December. Tamiris' *How Long, Brethren?*, combined with four of her *Negro Spirituals* rather than *Candide*, was revived on Broadway for a two week stand over the turn of the year. Even the ballet was recognized when in February 1938 Kirstein's Ballet Caravan was presented jointly by its management and the Federal Musical Theatre of New York, in conjunction with a Festival of American Music.[34] In the next April, Lily Mehlman's *Folk Dance of All Nations* was presented at the Hippodrome, while Tamiris produced her controversial *Trojan Incident*. Under the Federal Theatre also, in early 1939, Humphrey and Weidman presented a short run of three from their regular repertory, while, yet again, Tamiris produced, in a house with the barest of boards and the meanest of lights, another theatre piece, called *Adelante*, yet again on a controversial subject, Spain. A Federal dancers' entity was in evidence just when it was voted out of existence.[35]

Efforts were made by a few congressmen to save the Federal Theatre by setting up a permanent one in place of the temporary one under the WPA, but the still recalcitrant dancers who could never agree on the character of a temporary organization never rallied to the need for uniting on a permanent one either. For example, at a meeting in which Martha Graham read the official opinion of the American Dance Association in support of one of the pending congressional bills, she expressed her own personal opinion opposing it.[36]

By the time her *Adelante* was produced in April 1939, Tamiris had no company except the Federal Theatre dancers; she had no studio except the Federal Theatre rehearsal rooms. Her time and energy were spent traveling to Washington or conducting meetings in New York or reporting to the International Theatre Congress in Britain. Humphrey and Weidman had managed to keep their artistic entity, the Humphrey-Weidman Company, going throughout

---

[34] The program consisted of *Show Piece* (Erick Hawkins / Robert McBride), *Yankee Clipper* (Eugene Loring / Paul Bowles), and *Filling Station* (Lew Christensen / Virgil Thomson).
[35] Although the sources here on the Federal Theatre are many, no researcher can fail to acknowledge Grant Code's "Dance Theatre of the WPA: A Record of National Achievement" [*Dance Observer* 6 (Oct 1939) 264-65, 274; 6 (Nov 1939) 280-81, 290; and 7 (Feb 1940) 34-35] or Hallie Flanagan's *Arena* (New York: Duell, Sloan and Pearce 1940).
[36] The bill, admittedly not a perfect one, would have put power into the hands of the majority of dancers, of which, it was true, the modern concert dancers who had always run the project were only a small minority. The point is that, despite Tamiris' efforts, no group of dancers ever did agree on anything to substitute for the offending bill.

this period. One night their dancers would be dancing under their auspices, the next night under Federal Theatre. Wisely they felt financially unable to do Federal Theatre only. Tamiris was always too involved ever to be wise.

In summing up this stormy period of the Federal Theatre and the Federal Dance Theatre, one can note at length, as has been done necessarily, that the times were full of personal pique and passion, of bureaucratic inefficiency and insensitivity. But one can also say that it was a time of uncommonly good dance, even if one confines the judgment to the productions of Tamiris herself. In general, no production ever failed because of lack of quality of the choreography;[37] in especial, no production failed because of lack of quality of choreography on Tamiris' part.

Although an accurate accounting of the New York Project's productions has not been made, the following summary may provide perspective for an evaluation of Tamiris' artistic contribution to Federal Dance Theatre and Federal Theatre. The Humphrey-Weidman Company contributed the June 1936 Weidman *Candide* and Humphrey *Prelude, Parade,* and *Celebration* program, the May 1937 Weidman *Candide* half of the bill with Tamiris' *How Long, Brethren?*, and the January 1939 Humphrey *To the Dance, With My Red Fires,* and *Race of Life* program. All of these had been mounted previously for the Humphrey-Weidman Company; Humphrey-Weidman dancers were used in the Federal production. Ballet Caravan contributed the February 1938 *Show Piece, Yankee Clipper,* and *Filling Station* program. All dances had premiered previously and Ballet Caravan dancers were used in this cooperative occasion. The Young Choreographers Laboratory had a repertory season January through May 1937. Lily Mehlman's *Harvest Song* was one production, but other details on specific productions or dates are unavailable. The Young Choreographers Laboratory also presented the December 1937 matinees of Lily Mehlman's *Dances of All Nations,* Roger Pryor Dodge's *The Little Mermaid,* and Nadia Chilkovsky's *Mother Goose on Parade.* As far as is known, each was first mounted for the Federal Project. Lily Mehlman's number was presented a second time at the Hippodrome in April 1938. The ill-fated Becque had one production, *Young Tramps* of 1936, and Gluck-Sandor one, *The Eternal Prodigal* of December 1936. As far as is known, each was first mounted for the Federal Project, as was visiting artist Berta Ochsner's production, *Fantasy 1939* of June 1939. Nomada Johnson's *Bassa Moona,* presented by the Federal Music Project in Harlem, had some significant Negro dancing in it.

Tamiris contributed the July 1936 *Salut au Monde,* the May to July 1937 *How Long, Brethren?* with Weidman's *Candide,* the December 1937-January 1938 *How Long, Brethren?* and *Negro Spir-*

---

[37] For obvious evidence, there is Tamiris' award for group choreography from *Dance Magazine;* Lily Mehlman's *Harvest Song,* composed and first produced in the Young Choreographers Laboratory, received the best solo choreography of the season award at the same time.

ituals, the April 1938 play *Trojan Incident* (dance excerpts of which were also presented in Brooklyn), and the 1939 *Adelante*. All were mounted first for the Federal Project. An examination of these is necessary for a final evaluation of her contribution to Federal Theatre. Was Tamiris just the organizer, or did she contribute artistically as well? Were her compositions merely social action framed by a proscenium, or were they artistic entities? To answer these questions, it would be well to turn to an early evaluation of Tamiris by John Martin for orientation:

> Every so often one is brought up with a fresh start before the unique talent of the splendid young creature who calls herself Tamiris. One such moment occurred no longer ago than last Sunday night at the Guild Theatre when in the midst of a long and solemn suite called *Momentum* there burst upon the stage a radiant figure clad in burlesque Broadway trumpery, who with enormous gusto performed the choreographical equivalent of thumbing her nose at the tired business man's idea of diversion, and did it so delightfully that even the considerable number of apparently weary gentlemen of that character in the audience perforce applauded. That the solemnity of the suite could ever be restored after such a breath of vitality had blown upon the scene was out of the question; Tamiris had stolen the evening from herself.
>
> What a really thrilling dancer she is when she breaks free from the moorings of sobriety and lets what a European critic once called "the magnificent lust of motion" take possession of her! Long ago she stated her conviction of her dance as a dance of affirmation, and who is to contradict her? But it is none of your pious and self-conscious affirmations, dealing in noble principles and deathly truths; it is rather, the declaration of an entire delight in the dynamic actualities of the present, however wanting they may be in cosmic significance. That this is merely frivolous or wanton cannot be maintained in face of the dance itself, for it captures and brings to the surface that relish in living which most of us allow to be submerged all too easily in the welter of trying to get along. To be sure, we have our excuses, and good ones, but we are the losers, nevertheless.
>
> When Tamiris herself forgets to be affirmative and loses her native glow like any of the rest of us, there is cause for grieving. Why should she be bothered with denouncing and denying? There are plenty of vigorous minds outside the arts and an adequate number of stormy temperaments within them to take care thoroughly of denunciations and denials, but there are few indeed who have the gift of convincing us of our native exuberance and resiliency.

Martin closed his review with an analysis that gets to the heart of the Tamiris appeal:

> ... there is a vitality, a warmth, about her that relates her movements inevitably to human living, when she allows it to remain free from superimposed literary and philosophical dominance.... What we need from her is more and more of that affirmation upon which she has laid so much stress; and we need it not only because it is part and parcel of her art but also, since she is interested in "social content" in her dancing, because there is probably nothing anywhere to be found in the way of content that is more strongly social.

"Nothing anywhere to be found in the way of content that is more strongly social." The affirmation of life in all of its lusty grandeur—that is the heart of the art of Tamiris. To express this to the masses of people was the sense of mission of the woman Tamiris. Such was the art and the mission of Tamiris in the days of Federal Theatre.

Her first production, *Salut au Monde,* went directly to that affirmer of American life in all its ramifications, Walt Whitman. An opening solo by Tamiris was a greeting to the poet, uniting with him in a salute to the wide world. The middle three episodes of five, each introduced by a reader, depicted the struggle and disharmony among races despite the efforts of a few souls to create understanding. Lives of Chinese coolies, with their quiet acceptance of life, were contrasted with the lives of the American Negroes, with their boisterous challenge to life, in two dramatic scenes. Yet underneath, it was obvious Tamiris was saying, all have the same problems. The last episode returned to the theme of the opening affirmation as Tamiris in a solo exhorted her group to unite in peace and work together on a common earth.

In retrospect *Salut au Monde,* although triumphantly received as effective theatre, especially for the Federal Dance Theatre—the Brooklyn *Eagle* gave it first page coverage—is seen more now as an embryonic version of Tamiris' next Federal Dance Theatre production, *How Long, Brethren?.* Everyone, even at the opposite critical poles of the *Dance Observer* and the *Daily Worker,* agreed that *this* was a masterpiece. In form it was a simple suite of seven dances based on seven Negro songs of protest; a skeleton story, demarked by the songs *Pickin' off de Cotton, Upon de Mountain, Railroad, Scottsboro, Sistern an' Brethren, Let's Go to de Buryin',* and *How Long, Brethren?,* told of poverty, starvation, injustice, and death. The final song ended in a plea to change all this. A large Negro chorus and a full orchestra accompanied the dancers; all seemed welded together. Tamiris had found her historic theme, developed it to a striking climax, and ended it with hope, affirmation, "than which there is nothing more social."

In his review of this work, Martin delineated the extent of Tamiris' success artistically. He pointed out the difficulty for a choreographer to match music so rich and full as this, especially with a Negro choir to sing it. "Tamiris has met the situation well," he went on, "by making the choreography supplementary to the score, underlining its mood and intensity and adding a kind of stage counterpoint, without trying to overtop it or even to parallel it with action. As it is, frequently stage movement succeeds in spite of itself in topping music, notably in the exciting section called *Let's Go to de Buryin'* which is the high point of the evening." Again he found the affirmation of life in the Tamiris movement: "Tamiris' personal performance gives tremendous lift to the occasion," he wrote. "It is a delight to see movement characterized by freedom and continuity, especially now that these qualities are so rare."

The simple and honest movement and the eloquent design made the opening night audience stand up and cheer. In fact, the reaction was so wholehearted and spontaneous that the show was interrupted many times by applause and shouts so loud the dancers could not hear the orchestra or the chorus in the pit. Ovations throughout the unprecedented long run to standing-room-only crowds (the Federal Theatre thrived on statistics; the show played to 24,235 people) were nightly occurrences. Here was social comment on the dynamic actuality of the present that was artistic and popular. All agreed it was a splendid show that mirrored the Negro spirit and rhythm in the modern idiom. It was a statement of the here and now of the middle thirties, what *Hair* was to the late sixties.

The history of the production also included a revival at the end of 1936 and into early 1937. Instead of appearing with *Candide*, this production was preceded by four of Tamiris' plaintive *Negro Spirituals*, dances of slavery, resignation, and hope only in heaven. They turned out to be perfect to set the mood for the main piece, the dances of protest with their note of indignation and purpose not to wait for heaven for betterment. All agreed unanimously that this was one program in which Tamiris' glorious dancing was not expended on inept choreography. *Dance Magazine* gave her official recognition. Incidentally, she had also accomplished one of Becque's purposes for Federal Dance Theatre—the production of a full evening's work on a single theme.

If *How Long, Brethren?* was ecstatically acclaimed by everyone, *Trojan Incident*, Tamiris' next production for the Federal Project, was as passionately argued over. For this 1938 show, a script based on Euripides and Homer was prepared by a production group of the Federal Theatre; it included lines to be spoken as well as movement to be danced for Tamiris as Cassandra. In reality a short play concerned with the subjugation of Troy and the carrying off of its women into captivity, it nonetheless devoted half of its presentation to Tamiris and her group's dancing. A singing chorus in boxes on the stage added to the controversial set provided by Howard Bay.

One of the arguments over the effectiveness of the play was whether or not it was authentically Greek. Although it did not pretend to be —with its application to the social problems of the thirties, this use of the classics was attacked viciously. Today it might be seen as a precursor of the free application of the classics to present day conditions that is seen in such productions as *Dionysus '69*.

But the arguments about *Trojan Incident* made for good publicity, which the cast used to advantage in its advertisements: "There seems to be a difference of opinion," began the blurb's statement. The production was termed pretentious tommyrot, aesthetic whoopla and ordinary bunk, or a stimulating departure that achieved tremendous dramatic force. The music was taut, direct, and even pungently brutal, or shoddy and meaningless. The set, especially Bay's surrealistic bell, was absurdly silly or exceptionally beautiful. As to the dancing, Tamiris was accused of bringing such terrifying intensity to her movement both for herself and the group that it was claimed to be wearing on mind and spirit. Grant Code, in a defense of the work, called it the most vital resurrection of the Greek spirit he had ever seen. Divested of the dust of pseudo-classical scholasticism, it was not for those who lacked passion, pity, poetry, he wrote, nor for those who had not faith in life, a relish in living. It especially was not for the "smart so-what, ashamed of feeling anything real" crowd. John Martin identified her Cassandra's dance as a "mad, prophetic dance-song," "a strange, terrible dance" for which she had evolved "movements of power and conviction." In addition, she had achieved a "dozen glowing moments when the dancing lifts the scene into terms of universal emotions, transmuting the surface stuff of the Trojan myth into its underlying realities and touching into fire experiences of the mind as common to us as to the Greeks of twenty-five centuries ago."

After the play's short run, Tamiris, upon the demise of the Federal Theatre, did abstract her solo as Cassandra from the work and present it alone. About the deep and passionate sources of an artist's inspiration, it was a personal statement that embarrassed many. Certainly it was full of that affimation of life that Martin called social; perhaps it was too full, for the actualities of life Tamiris was facing personally, with the inevitable end of Federal Theatre, may have been too dynamic for her for once. The sentence at the end of Martin's review about the difficulties surrounding the production may also be taken as a comment upon Tamiris' life at the moment: "For the present it is perhaps enough to vote a laurel to Tamiris for a creative and imaginative piece of work against the most formidable of odds."

The odds were even greater against the success of the last production by Tamiris for Federal Theatre, for she had chosen the theme of Spain, that most controversial of countries during the thirties. One could easily be on the wrong side as the major nations divided and began the armament that led to the next war. Tamiris was not always on the right side; the production entitled *Adelante (Forward)* had to be changed many times before it was put on the bare boards of Daly's Theatre in April of 1939 and lit with the minimum of lighting. Shortly after it closed, the Federal Theatre Project was closed by act of Congress.

Margaret Lloyd in her *Borzoi Book of Modern Dance*[39] calls *Adelante* the first of the big modern ballets. One hour and fifteen minutes long, it was totally dance, with an off-stage voice in the role of a chorus used to hold the action together. Ten scenes or pictures of Spanish history and life, as visualized by a Loyalist soldier in moments of delirium between the shot of his execution and his death, led up to a Spain redeemed in the end.

The work has also been cited as important because it made no attempt to be authentically Spanish. Rather, the essence of Spain was sought and expressed in the modern idiom that was Tamaris' way of moving. John Martin went to see it on opening night and then was moved to return later. After his second visit when the lighting had improved to give it some theatrical magic, he recommended that his readers go see it, "unless you are distinctly blasé." He wrote of the troubles the production had had:

> *Adelante* has been through the wars: in this embattled period of the Federal Theatre, it has suffered cuts in personnel which necessitated patient adapta-

[39] (New York: Alfred A. Knopf, Inc 1949) p 145.

tion and, in what might be called the normal functioning of all relief projects, it has had to make replacements from time to time of dancers who found employment in other channels. But these are comparatively external difficulties. Planned a year ago when Spain presented quite a different face, it has also had to survive a major psychological change in its makeup. Nevertheless, with almost everything possible to interfere with it, it comes through now with dignity, conviction and integrity.

How, under such circumstances, a choreographer could produce a work of integrity is a measure of the human being Tamiris. "From the first, its conception was seen to be valid and dramatic," Martin continued. "Of the several works in extended form which Miss Tamiris has composed, none has achieved such a strong sequential line or been so tautly built. There is, to be sure, no specific plot, but there is a dramatic theme and it is well sustained even against the odds of a necessarily fragmentary pattern." Despite the use of such episodic material, Tamiris "has managed to hold it firmly together through the directness and persistence of its emotional line." Her own world was falling apart, but she was true to her sense of mission until the end.

Modern Program for National Dance Congress[40]

Fe Alf, Miriam Blecher, Gluck-Sandor, Sophie Maslow, Anna Sokolow, Felicia Sorel, Tamiris, Tamiris Group and Charles Weidman, Jose Limon and Bill Matons

May 23 1936   eve   New York: Kaufman Theatre (YMHA)

[*Combat* (Alf / Schwinghammer) Alf; *Ballad* (Sokolow / North) Sokolow; *Letter to the President* (Blecher / Moross) Blecher; *Paganini* (Gluck-Sandor / Kingsley) Gluck-Sandor; *Blues Trilogy* (Sorel / Kingsley) Sorel]; *Middle Ground* from *Harvest 1936* (Tamiris / Shostakovitch) Tamiris; *Nightriders* from *Momentum* (Tamiris / Howe) Tamiris Group; [*Two Songs About Lenin: In January He Died* and *In April He Was Born* (Maslow / Soviet Folk Songs) Mas-

---

[40] This and the following programs are taken from the published *Proceedings of the National Dance Congress*. On Wednesday evening, May 20 1936, The New Dance League ("both young zealots and restrained maturer artists," Margaret Lloyd summarized for the *Christian Science Monitor*) gave the following program:
  Greeting (/ Poulenc) Jose Limon and Letitia Ide; *March—Expulsion* (/ Prokofieff) Harry Losee; *Vigilantes* from *Inquisition, 1936* (Sokolow / North) Dance Unit; *Hymn* (Limon / percussion) Jose Limon; *Middle Class Portraits: Swivel Chair Hero* (Dudley / Honegger), *Dream-World Dora* (Dudley / Achron), *Aesthete* (Dudley / Honegger) and *Liberal* (Dudley / Prokofieff) Jane Dudley; *Chronicle (1935): Capture, Torment, Endurance* and *Conviction* (Delza /   ) Sophia Delza; *American Rhapsody* (/ Poem, Fearing) Bill Matons and Grusha Marek; *Dance In Three Parts* (Holm / Riegger): *A Cry Rises in the Land, Interlude,* and *New Destinies* Hanya Holm and Group; *Nostalgic Fragments* (/ Stravinsky): *March, Valse, Polka* and *Galop* Jose Limon and Letitia Ide; *Three Jewish Songs* (/ Achron) Lillian Shapero; *War Scene* from *Victory Ball* (Zemach / Schelling) Benjamin Zemach and Group; *Surrealiste Solemnity (1935)* (Delza / mutilated music of Prokofieff, Maliapiero, Casella, Gounod, Tschaikowsky, Antheil, Rubenstein, Bizet, Cassado, Youmans and Creston) Sophia Delza; *Four Soviet songs* (Sokolow / Adomian): *Sailors Holiday, Defend Our Land, Lullaby (Song about the stratosphere)* and *Sailors Chorus* Dance Unit
  Accompanists: Alex North, Charlotte Homer and Group from New Singers Chorus for the Dance Unit, Irma Jurist and Harvey Pollins for Hanya Holm and Group, Lillian Choen for Bill Matons, Estelle Parnas for Jane Dudley, Paul Creston for Sophia Delza, Norman Lloyd

Natl Dance Congress Program, cont
low; *Sea Gull* (Gluck-Sandor /   ) Gluck-Sandor; *Degradation* (Alf / Lissow) Alf; *Danzon* (Weidman / Debussy) Weidman; *Traditions* (Weidman / Engel) Weidman, Limon and Matons]

Accompanists: Genevieve Pitot and Aube Tzerke[41]; costumes for *Nightriders,* Rose Krupnick

Members of Tamiris Group: Helen Ayres, Ruth Baker, Rae Cohen, Ann Goodson, Nina Peters, Gertrude Peyser, Dvo Seron, Hilda Sheldon, Ida Soyer, Pearl Wall and Ray White

---

for Jose Limon and Letitia Ide, Herbert Kingsley for Harry Losee and Dora Brown, percussionist for Hanya Holm. Jack Riley read for Bill Matons

Of all the programs, most publicity was given to the big names of Martha Graham and Doris Humphrey who gave a Demonstration Program on Thursday Evening, May 21 1936:

Demonstration on Technique Graham and Group; *Educational Demonstration on Dalcroze Eurythmics* Paul Boepple and Group; *Lecture-Demonstration on Technique and Form* Doris Humphrey and Group: *On That Day* (Frances Leber / Honegger) and *D. A. R. (Red Scare No 1)* (Frances Leber / Debussy) Rebel Arts Dance Group; *Demonstration of Percussion with and without movement* Franziska Boas and Group; *Demonstration in Dance Method* Polly Korchien and Group; *Fugue* (Anita Zahn / Bach) and *Theme and Variations* (Anita Zahn / Corelli) Anita Zahn and Group

Martha Graham Group: Anita Alvarez, Bonnie Bird, Dorothy Bird, Ethel Butler, Lil Liandre, Marie Marchowsky, Sophie Maslow, May O'Donnell, Gertrude Shurr, Anna Sokolow and Kathleen Slagle

Piano, Dini de Remer

Paul Boepple Group: Margot Mayo, Alison Burroughs, Gabrielle Egger, Nettie Weissman, Johanne Gjerrulff, Mita Rom and Lola Rom

Doris Humphrey Group: Letitia Ide, Miriam Krakowsky, Joan Levy, Katherine Litz, Katherine Manning, Edith Orcutt, Beatrice Seckler and Sybil Shearer

Piano, Pauline Lawrence

Rebel Arts Dance Group: Sara Cohler, Rita Girden, Sarah Greenberg and Minna Kanfer

Piano, R. S. Ross

Franziska Boas Group: Melvene Ipcar, Nancy McKnight, Emily Hewlitt and Franziska Boas

Polly Korchien Group: Laurie Blankfort, Eva Darnova, Annabelle Green, Miriam Handelsman, Belle Isaacson, Elinor Ladd, Claudia Lewis, Bryne Miller, Hope Rochester, Dorothy Stone, Hope Svingarn and Naomi Westervelt

Piano, Harvey Brown

Anita Zahn Group: Rosemarie Beenk, Betty Friedman, Kathleen Hinn and Dorothy McDermid

Piano, Mary Shambaugh

Most of the theatre and variety dancers "didn't show," wrote Margaret Lloyd, for the Sunday evening, May 24 1936 Variety and Theatre Program. Those who did put on the following program:

Boogie-Woogie (/ Cleo Brown) Roger Pryor Dodge; *Weeping Mary* and *Git on Board Lil Chillun* (/ Burleigh) Edna Guy; *Promenade Amoureuse* (/ Lancier) Mura Dehn; *Night on Times Square* (/ Whithorne) and *Subway Angel* (/ A. Ellstein) Belle Didjah; *Gloomy Sunday* (/ Hungarian Suicide Song) and *Gavotte* (/ Bach) Anita Avila and Jack Nile; *The Man in the White Costume* (/ Anne Dodge) Roger Pryor Dodge and Group Mura Dehn, Glory Fortune, Betty Lea, Lea Samuels and Frances Selter; *Underground Printer* (/ German): *Illegal Pamphlets, Irresistible Protest* and *Peoples Front* and *Evolution of Power and Posture* (/ Pre-Man) John Bovingdon; *Yemenite Chant* (/ folk melodies) Belle-Didjah; *Fantasy Bolero* (/ De Falla) and *Tango* (/ Ravel) Anita Avila and Jack Nile

[The Bahaman Dancers called Motor Boat, Stew Beef, Alfred Sthran and John Oliver are listed as a group, but which number they danced is unidentified. Perhaps *Night on Times Square?*]

Accompanists: Anne Dodge for Dodge, [Gabriel Brown for Bahaman Dancers,] Eddy Barrie for Dehn, A. Pressman for Didjah, Geraldine Dansall and Sylvia Garner (singer) for Edna Guy and Isabelle Rich for Avila and Nile

[41] Accompanists: Alma Lissow for Alf, Sylvia Garner (singer) and Estelle Parnas for Blecher,

Federal Dance Theatre: Salut au Monde

July 23 1936 to Aug 5 1936   New York   Choreography and direction, Tamiris; music, Genevieve Pitot; text adaptation, Winthrop Parkhurst and John Bovingdon; reader, Arthur Spencer, courtesy of The Experimental Theatre

Salut au Monde, of all Whitman's poems, furnishes a prophetic insight into the problems of the American people and of the rest of mankind today. In it Whitman portrays Man the Individual, surrounded by nature and the environment created by his own efforts, struggling for his existence in the process of which he has created his crafts, his arts, his customs, his lands, his cities, his industries, his religions, his cultures and civilizations, his joys and sufferings— all that sustains man. And through all these innumerable forces and changes, he sees the divine right of the individual, regardless of race, sex, religion, country, social position, material wealth, or individual differences.

> Each of us inevitable,
> Each of us limitless—each of us with his or her right upon the earth,
> Each of us allow'd the eternal purports of the earth
> Each of us here as divinely as any is here.
>
> Walt Whitman, 1881 [42]

I

First Episode Tamiris; *Second Episode* group; *Third Episode, Part 1, 2, 3* group; *Fourth Episode* Tamiris with group; *Fifth Episode* Tamiris with group

Dancers in group: Marion Appel, Leah Berkowitz, Pauline Burbrick, Cecelia Fischer, Riva Katz, Ann Lief, Fanny Nassau, Lee Samuels, Selma Schneider, Jeanette Singer, Sasha Spector, Ida Teplan and Winifred Widener

II

Federal Theatre Negro Choral Ensemble. "Wen" Talbert, Director[43]

Piano, Genevieve Pitot and Roy Herbert; Federal Music Project Ensemble: flute, Louis Alberghini; clarinet, Salvatore Villanti; clarinet, Morris Beckerman; bassoon, Morris Gross; trumpet, Americe Caldena; tympanist, Samuel Feinbloom

---

Alex North and Simon Rady (singer) for Maslow, Herbert Kingsley for Gluck-Sandor and Sorel, Alex North for Sokolow and Ruth Lloyd for Weidman

[42] This introduction with the Whitman quotation was written by Tamiris for inclusion in the printed program.

[43] Two arranged spirituals: *Deep River* and *Steal Away* choral ensemble; *Can't You Hear Me Calling, Caroline* male choir with Charles Willis, soloist; Two traditional spirituals: *I Want to Be Ready* Olyve Hopkins and *Old Time Religion* choral ensemble with Millicent Holmes, soloist; *Old Man River* and *Sing No More* choral ensemble; *Dixie Moonlight* and *Rain, Rain, Rain* choral ensemble

Negro Choral Ensemble: Ruby Baker, Oscar Brooks, John Brown, James Davis, Laura Duncan, Horatio Edwards, Annie Gailard, Joseph Hall, Mae Haygood, Millie Holmes, Olyve Hopkins, Aldyth Louis, Hilda Manigault, Robert Moman, Ollie Parker, Nathlya Phillips, Henry Pittman, Frances Roame, S. Virginia Robinson, George Stevens, Dora Thompson and Charles Willis

Students' Dance Recitals, Washington Irving High School

Tamiris and her Group

Jan 16 1937   New York: Municipal Auditorium

Song of the Open Road 1st mvmt from *Walt Whitman Suite* Sydne Becker, Ida Tarvin and Ida Soyer; *Dirge* Tamiris; *Song of the Open Road* 3rd mvmt from *Walt Whitman Suite* Sydne Becker, Dvo Seron, Hilda Sheldon, Ida Soyer and Ida Tarvin; *Harvest 1935: Sycophants* Tamiris with Sydne Becker, Hilda Sheldon, Dvo Seron, Ida Soyer and Ida Tarvin; *Middle Ground* Tamiris and *Manouevers* Tamiris with Ada Abel, Sydne Becker, Ann Goodson, Alma Lass, Gertrude Peyser, Hilda Sheldon, Dvo Seron, Ida Soyer, Florence Ross, Ida Tarvin, Ray White and Pearl Wall; *Dance of Escape* Tamiris; *Legion* from *Momentum* Ada Abel, Sydne Becker, Vivian Cherry, Ann Goodson, Gertrude Peyser, Hilda Sheldon, Dvo Seron, Ida Soyer, Ida Tarvin, Ray White and Pearl Wall; *Flight* Tamiris; *Work and Play* [No 5] from *Toward the Light* Ada Abel, Sydne Becker, Gertrude Peyser, Ann Goodson, Hilda Sheldon, Dvo Seron, Ida Soyer, Ida Tarvin and Ray White; *Three Negro Spirituals: Swing Low, Sweet Chariot, Git on Board Lil Chillen* and *Joshua Fit de Battle ob Jericho* Tamiris; *South American Dance* Tamiris

Piano, Genevieve Pitot

New York Furriers Joint Council 25th Anniversary Concert

Tamiris and her Dance Group and others

Jan 23 1937   New York: Hippodrome Theatre   Benefit for Ladies Garment Workers Union

[*International* Freiheit Gesangs Verein; speech, Joseph Winogradsky, Chairman Jubilee Arrangement Comm; speech, Irving Potash, chairman; musical selections, Freiheit Gesangs Verein; violin selections, Eddy Brown; Yiddish Folk and Chassidic Presentations, singer—Victor Chenkin]; *Unemployed, Sh! Sh!, Legion, Night Riders, Diversion* and *Disclosure* from *Momentum* Tamiris and her Dance Group Ada Abel, Jilda Bronze, Sydne Becker, Rae Cohen, Vivian Cherry, Ann Goodson, Alma Lass, Gertrude Peyser, Florence Ross, Hilda Sheldon, Isabel Simon, Dvo Seron, Ida Soyer, Ida Tarvin, Pearl Wall and Ray White; [speeches, Pietro Lucchi and Ben Gold; Russian Folk and Soviet Presentations, Victor Chenkin; violin selections, Eddy Brown; *Operetta: A Bunt mit a Stachke* (E. Segal and L. Shapero / Jacob Schaeffer)]

Federal Dance Theatre, How Long, Brethren? *and* Candide

May 6 1937 to July 4 1937[44]   New York: Nora Bayes Theatre

WPA Federal Theatre Orchestra Conductor, Jacques Gottlieb; costume and setting execution, WPA Federal Theatre Workshop; production and lighting supervision, Stephen Karnot

I

How Long, Brethren? Choreography and Direction, Tamiris; music Genevieve Pitot, based on *Negro Songs of Protest*, Siegmeister-Gellert collection; costumes, James Cochrane. Episode I *Pickin' Off de Cotton* group; Episode II *Upon de Mountain* Tamiris with group; Episode III *Railroad* group, Episode IV *Scottsboro* group; Episode V *Sistern an' Brethren* group; Episode

---

[44] Grant Code wrote that the combined bill re-opened in New York in July at the Maxine Elliott Theatre with Ida Soyer in Tamiris' role and Philip Gordon in Weidman's. When it closed he does not state. Tamiris in her notes states that *How Long, Brethren?* had a total of 43 performances.

VI *Let's Go to de Buryin'* Tamiris with group; Episode VII *How Long, Brethren?* Tamiris with group

Dancers: Marian Appell, Leah Berkowitz, Pauline Bubrick, Cecelia Fisher, Augusta Gassner, Fanya Geltman, Ailes Gilmour, Margaret Kane, Riva Katz, Rose Levy, Fara Lynn, Lulu Morris, Fanny Nassau, Selma Schneider, Dvo Seron, Hilda Sheldon, Jeanette Singer, Sasha Spector and Ida Teplan

II

Candide Choreography and Direction, Charles Weidman.[45]

Dances for Spain

The New Dance Group (Miriam Blecher, director), Dance Unit (Anna Sokolow, director) and soloists Sophia Delza, Lasar Galpern, Lily Mehlman, Ruthanna Boris, Tamiris and Polonco Presented by the American Dance Association for the Medical Committee to aid Spanish Democracy

May 23 1937   New York: Adelphi Theatre

[*Gitanerias* (popular) Ruthanna Boris; *La Garterana* (popular) Ruthanna Boris; *Cape Dance* (traditional) Polonco; *Farucca* (traditional) Polonco]; *South American Dance* Tamiris; *Impressions of the Bull Ring* Tamiris; [*Renaissance Figure* (/ Leiberson) Sophia Delza; *We Weep for Spain* (/ de Falla) and *We March for Spain* (/ Chopin) Sophia Delza; *War to the End* (/ Albeniz) Lazar Galpern; *Farruca* (/ de Falla) Lazar Galpern; *Spanish Woman*: and *Lullaby for a Dead Child*(/ Creston) Lily Mehlman; *Flower Festival—Madrid, 1937* (Miriam Blecher /   Tolbie Sacher) New Dance Group; Excerpts from *A War Poem* (Sokolow / poem, F. T. Martinetti and music, Alex North) Dance Unit][46]

Federal Summer Theatre, Two Dance Suites[47]

July 10 1937   Poughkeepsie, NY: Vassar College

Prelude—Songs

Ezekiel Saw de Wheel, I Know I Have Another Building and *Walk in Jerusalem* Wen Talbert Choir with Singers Ruby Baker, Anne Gaillard, Dora Thompson, Hilda Manigault, Laura Duncan, Olive Hopkins, Charles Willis, George Stephens, Robert W. Moman, Horatio Edwards, James Dapus and John Brown

I

Swing Low, Sweet Chariot

Swing Low, Sweet Chariot (Tamiris / arr R. Johnson), *Git on Board Lil Chillun* (Ta-

---

[45] *Candide*, A Dance Interpretation of Voltaire's *Candide*. Principal Characters: Candide, Charles Weidman and Philip Gordon; Cunegonde, Lily Verne; Baron, Maurice Silvers; Baroness, Paula Bass and Bee Paris; Pangloss, Milton Feher; Paguette, Lily Mann; Priest, Philip Gordon and Lee Sherman; General, Add Bates; Martin, Sidney Stark; Jew, Lee Sherman; Cleric, Milton Feher; Don Fernando, Maurice Silvers

Dancers: Paula Bass, Add Bates, John Connolly, Peter Dominick, Milton Feher, Saida Gerrard, Mildred Gluck, Philip Gordon, Donald Knapp, Miriam Krakowsky, Irving Lansky, Ann Lief, Katherine Litz, Eve Lord, Lily Mann, Kathleen O'Brien, Bee Parris, Edith Pfefferman, Janet Schaff, Lee Sherman, Maurice Silvers, Ruth Sloan, Sidney Stark, Lily Verne and Winifred Widener

Choreography, Weidman; musical score, Wallingford Riegger and Genevieve Pitot; costumes and settings, Maxine Borowsky and Alexander Jones

[46] Order of program and members of groups not known.

[47] A program note identified this production as "The Federal Summer Theatre, made possible through the cooperation of the Works Progress Administration, the Rockefeller Foundation,

Two Dance Suites, cont
miris / arr Lawrence Brown), *Go Down Moses* (Tamiris / arr R. Johnson and R. Moman) and *Joshua Fit de Battle ob Jericho* (Tamiris / arr R. Johnson) Tamiris

II
How Long, Brethren?

Episode 1 *Pickin' Off de Cotton* ensemble; Episode 2 *Upon de Mountain* Tamiris and ensemble; Episode 3 *Railroad* ensemble; Episode 4 *Scottsboro* ensemble; Episode 5 *Sistern an' Brethren* ensemble; Episode 6 *Let's Go to de Buryin'* Tamiris and ensemble; Episode 7 *How Long, Brethren?* Tamiris and ensemble

Dancers: Marian Appell, Leah Berkowitz, Pauline Burbrick, Cecilia Fisher, Augusta Gassner, Fanya Geltman, Ailes Gilmour, Margaret Kane, Riva Katz, Rose Levy, Fara Lynn, Lulu Morris, Selma Schneider, Dvo Seron, Hilda Sheldon, Jeanette Singer and Sasha Spector

Choreography and direction, Tamiris; musical score, based on *Negro Songs of Protest* (Gellert-Siegmeister Collection), Genevieve Pitot; pianist, Genevieve Pitot; costumes, James Cochrane; songs sung by Wen Talbert Choir; lighting, Feder

The Federal Theatre Presents Tamiris

Tamiris and Dance Ensemble together with The Federal Theatre Negro Chorus in a Program of Dances and Songs

Dec 21 1937 to Jan 15 1938   eves   New York: 49th Street Theatre

I
The Federal Theatre Negro Chorus

Walk in Jerusalem, Just Like John, Ezekiel Saw the Wheel, I Know I Have Another Building, Hold On! Hold On! and *O, Mary, Don't You Weep! Don't You Moan!*

Director, Bob Moman

Singers: Ruby Baker, Oscar Brooks, John Brown, James Davis, Horatio Edwards, Anna Gaillard, Millie Holmes, Olyve Hopkins, Hilda Manigault, Natalya Phillips, Henry Pitman, Virginia Robinson, George Stephens, Dora Thompson and Charles Willis

II
Tamiris in Four Solo Dances

Swing Low, Sweet Chariot, Git on Board Lil Chillun, Go Down Moses, and *Joshua Fit de Battle ob Jericho*

Choreography, Tamiris; musical arrangement, Genevieve Pitot

III
How Long, Brethren?

Episode I *Pickin' Off de Cotton* ensemble; Episode II *Upon de Mountain* Tamiris and ensemble; Episode III *Railroad* ensemble; Episode IV *Scottsboro* ensemble; Episode V *Sistern an' Brethren* ensemble; Episode VI *Let's Go to de Buryin'* Tamiris and ensemble; Episode VII *How Long, Brethren?* Tamiris and ensemble

Choreography and direction, Tamiris; musical score, based on *Negro Songs of Protest* (Gellert-Siegmeister Collection), Genevieve Pitot; WPA Federal Theatre Orchestra with Jacques Gottlieb, conductor; costumes, James Cochrane; Songs sung by Federal Theatre Negro Chorus; lighting, Feder

Dancers: Mickey Appell, Ida Little, Leah Berkowitz, Fara Lynn, Pauline Bubrick, Lulu Morris, Cecilia Fischer, Lea Samuels, Augusta Gassner, Selma Schneider, Dvo Seron, Ailes Gilmour, Hilda Sheldon, Riva Katz, Jeanette Singer, Rose Levy, Sasha Spector and Ida Teplan

---

and Vassar College" and "a professional producing company of directors, actors, and designers from Federal Theatre units throughout the United States, who have been brought together for six weeks study and experimentation in the field of the theatre." The next production (July 29, 30 and 31 1937) was to be *1/3 of the Nation,* a new Living Newspaper production on the subject of housing.

Dance International 1900–1937 Presents
An Evening of Modern Dance

John Martin, Ruth St Denis, Martha Graham and Dance Group, Doris Humphrey and Charles Weidman and Dance Groups, Tamiris and Dance Group, Hanya Holm and Dance Group, and Louise Branch and the Dancers of the Nations

Jan 2 1938 eve   New York: Center Theatre

I
Introductory Remarks, John Martin

II
Ruth St Denis[48]

III
Martha Graham and Dance Group[49]

IV
Doris Humphrey and Charles Weidman and Dance Groups[50]

V
Momentum: Prelude—Unemployed, Sh! Sh!, Diversion—No 1, Sh! Sh!, Nightriders, Diversion—No 2 and *Coda* Tamiris with Ada Abel, Prudence Bredt, Jilda Bronze, Vivian Cherry, Rae Cohen, Alma Lass, Ida Little, Miriam Joseph, Bettina Mershon, Lilly Miller, Gertrude Peizer, Hilda Sheldon, Dvo Seron, Ida Soyer, Ann Weiner and Ray White

Musical direction, Genevieve Pitot; lighting, Robert Colman; costumes, Stephanie Klein and Edythe Gilfond.

VI
Hanya Holm and Dance Group[51]

VII
Louise Branch and the Dancers of the Nations

[48] *White Jade* (St Denis / Clifford Vaughn) St Denis; *Balinese Trio* (St Denis / Wells Hively) Anna Austin, Virginia Miller and Florence Lessing; *Black and Gold Sari* (St Denis / R. S. Stoughton) St Denis
   Musical direction, Louis Horst; costumes, Pearl Wheeler and Adolphine Rott
[49] *Frontier* American Perspective of the Plains (Graham / Louis Horst) Graham; *American Lyric* Dance of Assembly (Graham / Alex North) Martha Graham with May O'Donnell and Anna Sokolow and Dance Group Anita Alvarez, Thelma Babitz, Ethel Butler, Charlotte Chandler, Jane Dudley, Nelle Fisher, Frieda Flier, Nina Fonaroff, Natalie Harris, Marie Marchowsky, Sophie Maslow, Marjorie Mazia, Gertrude Shurr and Kathleen Slagle
   Musical direction, Louis Horst; decor for *Frontier,* Isamu Noguchi; costume direction for *American Lyric,* Edythe Gilfond
[50] *Theatre Piece* (Humphrey / Riegger): *Prologue—Assignment of Roles* Humphrey and group; *Behind Walls* Humphrey and group; *In the Open—Hunting Dance* Edith Orcutt, Charles Weidman and group; *Interlude* Humphrey; *In the Stadium* Jose Limon, George Bockman, Katherine Manning and group; *In the Theatre* Weidman, Katherine Manning and Katherine Litz; *The Race* Humphrey and group; *Epilogue—The Return* Humphrey and group
   Musical direction, Norman Lloyd; choreography for *In the Theatre,* Charles Weidman
   Members of the group: Katherine Manning, Joan Levy, Katherine Litz, Beatrice Seckler, Edith Orcutt, Sybil Shearer, Harriet Anne Gray, Eva Desca, Jose Limon, George Bockman, William Bales and Lee Sherman
[51] *Trend* (Holm / Riegger): *Mask Motions—Our Daily Bread* and *Satiety; Episodes* with Louise Kloepper as The Effete, Keith Coppage as Lucre Lunacy, Lucretia Wilson as From Heaven Ltd, Elizabeth Waters as Lest We Remember and Henrietta Greenhood as "he," the Great
   Setting and lighting, Arch Lauterer; costumes, Betty Joiner
   Members of Concert Group: Louise Kloepper, Lucretia Wilson, Carolyn Durand, Elizabeth

Dance for Spain

Ballet Caravan, Lincoln Kirstein, Director; Dance Unit, Anna Sokolow, Director; Paul Draper; Hanya Holm and Group; Martha Graham and Group; Arthur Mahoney; Tamiris and Group

Jan 28 1938   eve   New York: Hippodrome Theatre

I
Dance Unit, Anna Sokolow, Director[52]

II
Martha Graham and Dance Group[53]

III
Momentum: Prelude—Unemployed Ida Little, Dvo Seron, Hilda Sheldon and Ida Soyer, *Sh! Sh!* Tamiris, *Diversion—No 1* Ada Abel, Ida Little, Bettina Mershon, Gertrude Peyser, Dvo Seron, Hilda Sheldon, Ida Soyer, Ann Weiner and Ray White, *Sh! Sh!* Tamiris, *Nightriders* Ada Abel, Tilda Bronze, Miriam Joseph, Alma Lass, Ida Little, Bettina Mershon, Lillian Nash, Gertrude Peyser, Pauline Subin, Dvo Seron, Hilda Sheldon, Ida Soyer, Ann Weiner and Ray White, *Diversion—No 2* Tamiris and *Coda* Ada Abel, Tilda Bronze, Miriam Joseph, Alma Lass, Ida Little, Bettina Mershon, Lillian Nash, Gertrude Peyser, Pauline Subin, Dvo Seron, Hilda Sheldon, Ida Soyer, Ann Weiner and Ray White

Pianos, Genevieve Pitot and Herbert Haufreucht; costumes, Stephanie Kline; costumes for *Diversion No 1*, Edythe Gilfond; music for *Diversion No 2*, Armstrong

IV
Address by Mr Martin Wolfson

V
Hanya Holm, her Concert Group and an augmented dance group[54]

Waters, Henrietta Greenhood, Keith Coppage, Marva Spelman, Miriam Kagan and Harriet Roeder
   Members of augmented group: Valerie Bettis, Franziska Boas, Katherine Sue Bolte, Uwarda Egley, Helen Ellis, Gerris Gerow, Mary Gillette, Dorothea Hanwell, Barbara Hatch, Hildegarde Just, Ruth Ledoux, Caroline Locke, Sarah McRoberts, Jane Perry, Jeanette Sauborn, Elizabeth Sherbon, Sydia Tarnower, Josephine Taylor, Jane Wright, Collin Wilsey and Julia Anne Wilson
[52] Excerpts from *A War Poem* (Sokolow / poem, F. T. Marinetti and music, Alex North) a *War is Beautiful,* b *War is Beautiful because it fuses Strength, Harmony and Kindness,* c *War is Beautiful because it realizes the long dreamed-of metalization of the human body,* d *War is Beautiful because it symphonizes pauses choked by silence, the perfumes and odors of putrification, and creates the spiral smoke of burning villages,* and e *War is Beautiful because it serves the greatness of our great Fascist Italy.* Dance Unit
   Members of the Dance Unit: Aza Cefkin, Ronya Chernia, Frances Hellman, Ruth Freedman, Rose Levy, Grusha Mark, Mary Monroe, Ruth Nissenson, Florence Schneider, Sascha Spector, Lew Rose, Allen Wayne, Michael Gray and Martin Michel
   Pianos, Alex North and Jesus Duron; percussion, Sam Prizant; costumes, Anton Refregier
[53] *Imperial Gesture—A Study in Arrogance* (Graham / Lehman Engel) Graham; *Celebration—Dance of Rejoicing* (Graham / Louis Horst) Dance Group; *Deep Song* (Graham / Henry Cowell) Graham
   Dance Group: Anita Alvarez, Thelma Babitz, Ethel Butler, Nelle Fischer, Frieda Flier, Nina Fonoroff, Marie Marchowsky, Sophie Maslow, Marjory Mazia, May O'Donnell, Gertrude Shurr and Kathleen Slagle
   Piano, Louis Horst
[54] Extracts from *Trend: The Gates Are Desolate* (Holm / Riegger), *Resurgence* (Holm / Varese) and *Assurance* (Holm / Varese) Holm, her Concert Group and an augmented dance group
   Concert Group Members: Louise Kloepper, Lucretia Wilson, Carolyn Durand, Elizabeth

Tamiris and Her Sense of Mission, 1936-1939

VI
Paul Draper[55]

VII
The Ballet Caravan, Lincoln Kirstein, Director[56]

VIII
Arthur Mahoney[57]

Federal Theatre, Trojan Incident

Apr 21 1938 to May 21 1938   New York: St James Theatre

Adaptation from Homer and Euripides, Philip H. Davis and production staff; producer, Dillard Long; staging, Harold Bolton and Tamiris; design, Howard Bay; music, Wallingford Riegger; choral group conductor, Genevieve Pitot; WPA Federal Theatre Orchestra conductor, Wallingford Riegger.

Prologue—Tent of Odysseus; The Plain outside Troy

Odysseus, Marcel Roussenu; Agamemnon, Frank Curran; Menelaus, Joseph Kramm; Thersites, Michael Cisney; Talthybius, Colfax Sanderson; Hecuba, Isabel Bonner; First Woman, Susanne Remos; Second Woman, Hilda Sheldon; Third Woman, Paula Bass; Fourth Woman, Augusta Gassner; Fifth Woman, Dvo Seron; Sixth Woman, Lea Samuels; Seventh Woman, Mildred Albert; Eighth Woman, Rose Levy; Ninth Woman, Kathleen O'Brien; Tenth Woman, Mildred Tanzer; Cassandra, Tamiris; First Soldier, Edward Segal; Andromache, Jane Taylor; Astyanax, Peggy Romano; Attendant, Willie Kaufman; Helen, Evelyn Swenson Eden; Women of Troy: Marion Appel, Pauline Bubrick, Lily Faber, Saida Gerrard, Riva Katz, Ida Little, Valentine Litvinoff, Fara Lynn, Lulu Morris, Edith Pfefferman and Gertrude Wasinsky. Choral group: Ruby Baker, Wallace Banfield, Phyliss Bolce, Willis E. Bradley, Oscar Brooks, John Brown, James Davis, Laura Duncan, Anna Gaillard, Ray Holland, Millie Holmes, Hilda Manigault, Bob Moman, Natalya Phillips, Henry Pittman, Virginia Robinson, Agnes Sanford, George Stephens, Ada May Talbot, Dora Thompson, Lillian Wartell, Charles Willis and Maud Ward

Waters, Henrietta Greenhood, Keith Coppage, Marva Spelman, Miriam Kagan and Harriet Roeder

Members of the augmented group: Valerie Bettis, Franziska Boas, Katherine Sue Bolte, Uwarda Egley, Helen Ellis, Gerrie Gerow, Mary Gillette, Dorotheat Hanwell, Barbara Hatch, Hildegarde Just, Ruth Ledoux, Caroline Locke, Sarah McRoberts, Jane Perry, Jeanette Saurborn, Elizabeth Sherbon, Lydia Tarnower, Josephine Taylor, Jane Wright, Collin Wilsey and Julia Anne Wilson

Setting and lighting, Arch Lauterer; costumes, Betty Joiner

[55] *Minuet* (Draper / Handel), *Ain't Necessarily So* (Draper / Gershwin) and *Blue Danube Waltz* (Draper / Strauss) Paul Draper

Piano, David Le Winter

[56] *Show Piece* (Erick Hawkins / Robert McBride): *Preliminaries* Eugene Loring, *Parade* ensemble, *Little Scherzo* Ruby Asquith, *Strut* Ruby Asquith, Mary Heater and Lorna London, *Jig* Douglas Coudy, *Pizzicato* Albia Kavan, *Heroic Air* Lew Christensen, *Bolero* Jane Doering, *Pantomime and Imitation* Eugene Loring and ensemble, *Waltz* Marie Jeane and Fred Danieli, *Nightmare* Marjory Moore, *Threesome and Foursome* ensemble, *Grand Adagio* Marie Jeane and Fred Danieli and *Workout and Finale* ensemble

Piano, Trude Rittman; costumes, Keith Martin

[57] *Farruca* and *Medias* (/ Music Popular) Arthur Mahoney. Guitar, Villarino

Works Progress Administration Federal Arts Projects of New York, A Night of The Arts: Gala Spring Festival

Various Arts Projects Companies, including Tamiris and Thirty Dancers

Apr 25 1938   eve   Brooklyn: Academy

[Musical selections by The New York Civic Orchestra, Eugene Plotnikoff, conductor; Debate Scene from *Prologue to Glory* Stephen Courtleigh, Ann Rutledge and a cast of forty from the Theatre Project; Skit *Mirror to America* by Writers Project with Theatre Project Cast;] *Trojan Incident* Tamiris and thirty dancers from Theatre Project; [musical selections by The New York Civic Orchestra]

Students' Dance Recitals, Washington Irving High School

Tamiris, assisted by Ida Soyer, Ida Little and Bettina Mershon

Nov 12 1938   eve   New York: Municipal Auditorium

Dirge, Flight, Cassandra's Dance from *Trojan Incident, Impressions of the Bull Ring* and *South American Dance* Tamiris; *Negro Spirituals* Tamiris, Ida Soyer, Ida Little and Bettina Mershon[58]

Piano, Genevieve Pitot; singers, Dora Thompson and Bob Moman

Second Annual Dance for Spain

Doris Humphrey and Charles Weidman, Martha Graham, Tamiris, Arthur Mahoney and Thalia Mara, Edwin Michaels, Anna Sokolow, Juan Martinez and Antonita and Felicia Sorel

Sponsored by the American Dance Association for the Medical Bureau, and North American Committee to Aid Spanish Democracy

Feb 5 1939[59]   eve   New York: Mecca Temple

[*To the Dance* (Humphrey-Weidman / arr Norman Lloyd) Humphrey, Weidman and Group Katherine Manning, Letitia Ide, Katherine Litz, Beatrice Seckler, Harriette Anne Gray, Eva Desca, Gloria Garcia, Marice Maginnis, José Limon, George Bockman, William Bales and Lee Sherman; *Traditions* (Weidman / Lehman Engel) Weidman with José Limon and George Bockman; *Frontier* (Graham / Louis Horst) Graham;] *Diversion* from *Momentum* Tamiris; [*Alegrias* Mara, *Farruca* Mahoney, *Media Granadinas* (guitar solo) Jeronimo Villarino and *Sevillanas* Mahoney and Mara: *The Marionette Stage* from *Pinocchio* with Michaels as Pinocchio, Gabrielle Duval as Ballerina, George Cohan as Warrior and Helen Galuback as Rag Doll; *Slaughter of the Innocents* (Sokolow / Alex North) Sokolow;] *Negro Spirituals: Go Down Moses, Swing Low, Sweet Chariot, Git on Board Lil Chillen* and *Joshua Fit de Battle ob Jericho* Tamiris with singers Dora Thompson and Bob Moman; *Cordova(/ Classic)* and *Meu Meco*

---

[58] This program has been put together incompletely from reviews. An accurate program is unavailable.

[59] There is evidence that Tamiris and her Group appeared in the Students' Dance Recitals at the Washington Irving High School on Feb 25 1939; no program is available.

Tamiris and Her Sense of Mission, 1936-1939

(/ Flamenco) Martinez and Antonita; *Railroad Work Dance* (Sorel / songs, Fred Stewart, choral arr Lehman Engel)⁶⁰ Dorothy Bird, Jenifer Chatfield and Peggy Ann Holmes as Fancy Ladies, Kathleen Slagle as Watercarrier, Bill Benner, Robert Breen, Phil Brown, James G. Burrell, Melchor Ferrer, William Howell, William Matons, Frank Maxwell, Frank Westbrook, Charles S. Clarke, John Dickens, Judson Best Hall, Meredith Johnson, Fred Stewart, Jon Urban and Earl Weatherford as Railroad Workers, Eleanor Knapp and Louise Virden as Singers and Tony Kraber as Singer and Guitarist]

Pianists: [for Humphrey and Weidman, Lionel Nowak; for Graham, Louis Horst;] for Tamiris, Genevieve Pitot [for Sokolow, Alex North; for Martinez and Antonita, Ward Harris. Guitarists: for Mahoney and Mara, Jeronimo Villarino and for Sokolow, Jules Wexler]

Federal Theatre, Adelante

Apr 20 1939 to May 6 1939   New York: Daly's Theatre

A Dance Production on a Spanish Theme by Helen Tamiris; music, Genevieve Pitot; Spanish translation of poems, Eli Siegel and Rolfe Humphries; additional verse, Bob Whittington; sets and costumes, Alexander Jones; narration direction, Brett Warren; lighting, Harry Peters; producer, Charles K. Freeman; chorus director, Genevieve Pitot; WPA Federal Theatre Orchestra conductor, Wallingford Riegger; dance coordinator, Evelyn David

In *the Plaza; Transition; The Court: On the Balcony* and *In the Court; Love's Dance; Chant for the Dead; In the Church; In the Village; With the Generals; Strange Encounter: Lady with the Fan* and *Recognition; Transition; Finale*

Peasant Soldier, Bill Matons; His Beloved, Helen Tamiris; Narrator, Alfredo Allegro; Peasant men and women, soldiers, generals, courtiers, ladies: Paula Bass, Pauline Bubrick, Florence Cheasnov, Mura Dehn, Fanya Geltman, Ailes Gilmour, Ida Little, Lulu Morris, Klarna Pinska, Vivian Manet, Selma Rubin, Hilda Sheldon, Janet Schaff, Selma Schneider, Alex Tairoff, Mildred Tanzer, Roger Dodge, Donald Knapp, Rajah O'Hardino, Richard McMurray, Marvin Marzoff and Al Rosenblum

International House Performance

The American Dancer Helen Tamiris, assisted by Ida Soyer, Ida Little and Sydne Becker

July 29 1939   eve   New York: The Auditorium   Presented by Grant Code

My Call Is the Call of Battle (Tamiris / Pitot) Sydne Becker, Ida Little and Ida Soyer; *Dirge* Tamiris; [*Lost Spring* (Soyer / Berenice Stone) Ida Soyer;] *Twentieth Century Bacchante* Tamiris; *Flight* Tamiris; Negro Spirituals: *Go Down Moses* Tamiris, [*Ezekiel Saw de Wheel* (Soyer /   ) Ida Soyer, *It's Me, O Lord* (Little /   ) Ida Little,] *Swing Low, Sweet Chariot* Tamiris, *Git on Board Lil Chillen* Tamiris, [*Wade in de Water* (Soyer and Little /   ) Sydne Becker, Ida Little and Ida Soyer] and *Joshua Fit de Battle ob Jericho* Tamiris; [*War Face* (Soyer / Berenice Stone) Ida Soyer;] *Cassandra's Dance* from *Trojan Incident* (Tamiris / Wallingford Riegger) Tamiris; *Diversion* from *Momentum* Tamiris; *South American Dance* Tamiris; *Impressions of the Bull Ring* Tamiris

Piano, Genevieve Pitot; singers, Dora Thompson and Bob Moman

---

⁶⁰ *Railroad Work Dance* was from Marc Connolly and Bela Blau's production of *Everywhere I Roam* by Arnold Sundgaard and Marc Connolly, original costumes by Robert Edmond Jones.

Third Annual Stars for Spain Program

Dec 10 1939   eve   New York: Mecca Temple   Benefit for Dorothy Parker's Spanish Refugee Children's Fund, under auspices of Spanish Refugee Relief Campaign

[Wilbert Griffith and his Harlem Swing Club Orchestra; Jack Guilford, Boogie-Woogie Pianists and Hazel Scott, all courtesy Cafe Society with Glenn Anders, Master of Ceremonies; *Javanese Porcelain* (/ Edgar Stillman Kelley) and *Rhapsody in Blue* (/ Gershwin) Maria Gambarelli; Monty Wooley, Paul Draper and Eddie Dowling; The Little Group in *Darryl Zanuck Goes With The Wind* by Sam Locke with Jane Hoffman, Frances Dworkin, Ann Blair, Billy Carr, Paul Roberts, Leon Rose and Arno Tanny, Elsie Peters at the piano; Theme Song from *No for an Answer* by Marc Blitzstein with Michael Loring, Marc Blitzstein at the piano; Philip Merivale; Gypsy Rose Lee and Lionel Stander; Wilbert Griffith and his Harlem Swing Club Orchestra; *Songs of Republican Spain* Consuela Moreno; Margo and Herbert Rudley from *The World We Make* with Hiram Sherman, Master of Ceremonies; *Deep Song* (Graham / Cowell) Graham with Horst at the piano; *Vive La France* Ruth Draper; *Waiting for Odets* from the New Theatre League Collection 1939 with Roman Bohnen, Phoebe Brand, Morris Carnovsky, Lee Cobb, Philip Loeb, Ruth Nelson and Art Smith;] [*To a Tired Business Man*] *Diversion* from *Momentum* Tamiris with Genevieve Pitot at the piano; [Molly Picon with A. Ellman at the piano; *The Hobo* (/ David Guion) Valya Valentinoff with Alex North at the piano; *Ballad for Americans* by E. Robinson and John LaTouche sung by the American People's Chorus, "Uncle Sam" sung by Michael Loring, with Earl Robinson at the piano]

5 Tamiris' Studio Theatre, 1940–1944

WITH THE DEMISE of the Federal Theatre, Tamiris had nowhere to go. Other major dancers had kept their companies together, their studios in operation, while tours extended their reputations. In 1940, Tamiris, now publicly Helen Tamiris (to add respectability?), had nothing. Worst of all, she was suspect politically. Proud at the time, in the early thirties, of dancing for a benefit of the *New Masses* or with the Major Revolutionary Workers' Dance League, she now found herself thought of as a Red. Giving her all to the Federal Theatre in the late thirties, she found, upon its disappearance, many thought she had been foolish to work so hard for so shoddy an organization. Now it was no longer fashionable to be poor; the country was becoming rich as the approaching war gave a boost to the economy.

Indeed, she found that her imaginative organization, the American Dance Association, was naive in comparison with the unions that now moved in and signed up dancers—for wages no independent choreographer could pay. In short, all of her activities which had been sincere responses to the needs of the times were out of date. Tamiris was a hasbeen with a Red reputation in a country that had not yet teamed up with the Communists. For once, she was out of step—not in tune with her era.

On top of all this, the moderns, who had loudly declared and proved throughout the past decade that ballet was dead, found a very much alive corpse around. Having believed that the new modern dance was to be *the* dance in rough and robust America, its leaders faced the fact, on the eve of the war, that ballet was the dance receiving the support of Americans. Lincoln Kirstein doggedly backed George Balanchine until this choreographer and his style of ballet moved into the center of the dance world; Lucia Chase poured her wealth into American Ballet Theatre (called by various titles during its life) until its style of ballet, American perhaps, became recognized.

The moderns were forced, in a sense, to go underground. Unable to pay union wages or union houses, they developed their own studios into little theatres that could be used for both studios to teach in and theatres to perform in. All, except Martha Graham who continued to produce her works in theatres, were forced to establish these makeshift theatres and produce their works in what would today be called Off-Broadway.

Pulling herself together as well as she could, Tamiris found a large basement on Lafayette Street for her studio-theatre. A stage was simply demarked on the floor by two pylons which housed the lights; raised seats made a hundred and twenty-five places for the audiences, with room for perhaps twenty-five more to stand. There her devoted followers came.

Gradually, Tamiris sensed the change in the climate of America and began to react again. A transitional dance, *As in a Dream*, the title of which suggested its choreographer's condition, soon gave way to a flamboyant *Floor Show*, the title of which stated its choreographer's intention. Broadway producers were looking for light and gay escapist fare as the war swept the country completely. Tamiris would attract bookings where the money was by producing satiric pieces designed to appeal to the paying customers of the cabarets. But to both herself and the producers who came, the falseness was evident. It was only when she turned to material that had always been hers natively that she produced a work of sincerity—and excellence. She, in reality, returned to the "Manifest" of her early years in which she had written, "Sincerity is based on simplicity. A sincere approach to art is always done through simple forms." The two dances that revealed the true Tamiris with her great affirmative posture were *Liberty Song* and *Bayou Ballads*, both based on songs of native America. These, ironically, proved to be the the dances which attracted the night club managers such as John Roy of the Rainbow Room in Radio City. Tamiris, by being her sincere self, by reacting to the needs of a new moment, was again being modern.

Another example of her sensitivity to the times was her choreography for a play for the United States Department of Agriculture. Designed to popularize meat rationing during the war, the production *It's Up to You* was given in cooperation with the Skouras Theatres, the American Theatre Wing and the Food Industries. As Porterhouse Lucy, the Black Market Steak, Tamiris opened at a gala event in Washington, D.C. before the Secretary of Agriculture, then toured in that city and in New York City. Later she and her new company, including her husband Daniel Nagrin, were part of a revue entitled *The People's Bandwagon*, put together for appearances in movie theatres for the purpose of reelecting Franklin D. Roosevelt in 1944. "The exciting thing about this tour," Tamiris recalled, "was the knowledge that the dance could be part of something as important as helping to elect a president. We [Daniel Nagrin and herself] not only did some of our own concert dances but appeared in especially created material on the election." Tamiris had recovered; soon she would achieve her goal—Broadway.

Students' Dance Recitals, Washington Irving High School

Helen Tamiris and her Group, assisted by Philip Gordon

Jan 27 1940   eve   New York: Municipal Auditorium

Negro Spirituals: Go Down Moses Tamiris, [*Ezekiel Saw the Wheel* Ida Soyer, *It's Me, It's Me, Oh Lord* Ida Little,] *Swing Low, Sweet Chariot* Tamiris; *Git on Board Lil Chillen* Tamiris; [*Wade in de Water* Sydne Becker, Ida Soyer and Ida Little] and *Joshua Fit de Battle ob Jericho* Tamiris; *How Long, Brethren? Upon de Mountain, Scottsboro, Let's Go to the Burial* and *How Long, Brethren?* Tamiris and group; [*For the Tired Business Man*] *Diversion* from *Momentum* Tamiris; *Last Spring* Ida Soyer; *Adelante: In the Court—Pavane, Love's Song, In the Court—Masks, Lady with the*

Tamiris' Studio Theatre, 1940-1944

Fan and *In the Village* Tamiris and group; *Kentucky Gal* Tamiris[61]

Piano, Genevieve Pitot; singers, Laura Duncan, Hilda Manigault and Bob Moman

Tamiris Studio Theatre Recital

Helen Tamiris and Group

Dec 7 and 14 1940   eves   New York: Tamiris Studio Theatre

[*For the Tired Business Man*] *Diversion* from *Momentum* Tamiris; *These Yearnings, Why Are They?* (Tamiris / Pitot) Sydne Becker, Ida Little and Ida Soyer; *Dirge* Tamiris; [*Love Duet*] *Love's Dance* from *Adelante* Tamiris with Philip Gordon; *Lady with the Fan* from *Adelante* Tamiris with Philip Gordon; *Song of Today* (Tamiris / Pitot) Tamiris; *Floor Show: We Present* (Tamiris / Pitot) Erik Walz as Master of Ceremonies and Tamiris, Sydne Becker, Bettina Harris, Ida Little and Ida Soyer as Entertainers, *Sister Act* (Harris and Little / arr Pitot) Bettina Harris and Ida Little, *Tres, Tres Elegante* (Tamiris / Pitot) Tamiris with Eric Walz, *Honky Tonk* (Tamiris / Pitot) Tamiris with Bettina Harris and Ida Little, *Orientalia* (Tamiris / Pitot) Ida Soyer, Ida Little and Erik Walz, *Seventh Girl from the Left* (Tamiris / Pitot) Tamiris, *Dumb Show* (Tamiris / Pitot) Sydne Becker and Erik Walz, *Four Torches* (Tamiris / Pitot) Tamiris with Bettina Harris, Ida Little and Ida Soyer and *Finale* (Tamiris / Pitot) Tamiris with Sydne Becker, Bettina Harris, Ida Little, Ida Soyer and Erik Walz

Piano, Genevieve Pitot

Tamiris Studio Theatre Recital

Helen Tamiris and Group

Feb 2, 9, 16 1941   eves   New York: Tamiris Studio Theatre

Negro Spirituals: Go Down Moses Tamiris, [*Ezekiel Saw the Wheel* Ida Soyer, *It's Me, It's Me, Oh Lord* Ida Little,] *Swing Low, Sweet Chariot* Tamiris, *Git on Board Lil Chillen* Tamiris [*Wade in de Water* Sydne Becker, Ida Soyer and Ida Little,] *Joshua Fit de Battle ob Jericho* Tamiris, *Crucifixion* Tamiris and *When the Saints Go Marchin' In* (Tamiris /   ) Tamiris with group; *Song of Today* Tamiris; *As in a Dream: Withdrawal, The Vanished, Vain Pursuit, Duality* and *Return* (Tamiris / Pitot) Tamiris with group; *Floor Show: We Present, Sister Act, Tres, Tres Elegante, Honky Tonk, Orientalia, Seventh Girl from the Left, Dumb Show, Four Torches* and *Finale* Tamiris with Sydne Becker, Bettina Harris, Ida Little, Ida Soyer and Erik Walz

Piano, Genevieve Pitot; costumes for *As in a Dream*, Liz Reitell; singers for *Negro Spirituals*, Dora Baker, Dora Thompson and Bob Moman

Students' Dance Recitals, Washington Irving High School

Helen Tamiris and Group

Mar 15 1941   eve   New York: Municipal Auditorium

Negro Spirituals: Go Down Moses Tamiris, [*Ezekiel Saw the Wheel* Ida Soyer, *It's Me, It's Me, Oh Lord* Ida Little,] *Swing Low, Sweet Chariot* Tamiris, *Git on Board Lil Chillen* Tamiris, [*Wade in de Water*, Sydne Becker, Ida Soyer and Ida Little,] *Joshua Fit de Battle ob Jericho* Tamiris, *Crucifixion* Tamiris and *When the Saints Go Marchin' In* Tamiris with group; *Song of Today* Tamiris; [*Brief Victory* (Ida Soyer / Berenice Stone) Ida Soyer;] *As in a Dream: Withdrawal, The Vanished, Vain Pursuit,*

---

[61] This program has been put together incompletely from reviews. An accurate program is unavailable.

Students' Dance Recitals, cont
Duality and *Return* Tamiris with group; *Floor Show: We Present, Sister Act, Tres Tres Elegante, Honky Tonk, Orientalia, Seventh Girl from the Left, Dumb Show, Four Torches* and *Finale* Tamiris with Sydne Becker, Bettina Harris, Ida Little, Ida Soyer and Erik Walz

Piano, Genevieve Pitot; costumes for *As in a Dream* and *Negro Spirituals*, Liz Reitell; singers for *Negro Spirituals*, Dora Baker, Dora Thompson and Bob Moman

Tamiris Studio Theatre Recital

Helen Tamiris and Group

Apr 20, 27 1941   eves   New York: Tamiris Studio Theatre

Negro Spirituals: Go Down Moses Tamiris; [*Ezekiel Saw de Wheel* Ida Soyer; *It's Me, It's Me, Oh Lord* Ida Little,] *Swing Low, Sweet Chariot* Tamiris, *Git on Board Lil Chillen* Tamiris, [*Wade in de Water* Sydne Becker, Ida Soyer and Ida Little,] *Joshua Fit de Battle ob Jericho* Tamiris, *Crucifixion* Tamiris and *When the Saints Go Marchin' In* Tamiris and group; *Liberty Song* (Tamiris / songs of American Revolution, arr Pitot): *What a Court Hath Old England* Tamiris with Sydne Becker, Bettina Harris, Ida Soyer, Gilda Bronze, Judy Jaffe and Erik Walz or Paul Seymour, *My Days Have Been So Wondrous Free* Tamiris with Erik Walz or Paul Seymour, *Bunker Hill* Tamiris with Bettina Harris, Ida Soyer, Paul Seymour and Erik Walz and *Ode to the Fourth of July* Tamiris with Ida Soyer, Sydne Becker, Bettina Harris, Ann Wilson, Judy Jaffe, Gilda Bronze, Erik Walz and Paul Seymour

Piano, Genevieve Pitot; percussions, Jack Wolf; costumes for *Negro Spirituals*, Liz Reitell and for *Liberty Song*, Rhoda Rammelkamp; singers for *Negro Spirituals* Laura Duncan, Dora Thompson and Bob Moman and for *Liberty Song* Isabelle Josephs, Evelyn Stern, Saul Samuelson and Arthur Barrie

Tamiris Studio Theatre Recital

Helen Tamiris and Group

Jan 11, 18, 25 1942   eves   New York: Tamiris Studio Theatre

Liberty Song: What a Court Hath Old England Tamiris with Sydne Becker, Bettina Harris, Ida Soyer, Gilda Bronze, Judy Jaffe and Maurice Silvers, *My Days Have Been So Wondrous Free* Tamiris and Daniel Nagrin, *Bunker Hill* Tamiris with Bettina Harris, Ida Soyer, Paul Seymour and Daniel Nagrin and *Ode to the Fourth of July* Tamiris with Sydne Becker, Gilda Bronze, Vivian Cherry, Bettina Harris, Judy Jaffe, Ida Soyer, Maurice Silvers and Daniel Nagrin; *Negro Spirituals:* [*Wade in the Water* Bettina Harris, Ida Little and Ida Soyer,] *Go Down Moses* Tamiris, [*Ezekiel Saw de Wheel* Ida Soyer, *It's Me, It's Me, O Lord* Ida Little,] *Swing Low, Sweet Chariot* Tamiris, *Git on Board Lil Chillen* Tamiris, *Joshua Fit de Battle ob Jericho* Tamiris, *Crucifixion* Tamiris and *When the Saints Go Marchin' In* Tamiris with Vivian Cherry, Bettina Harris, Ida Little and Ida Soyer; *Good-Will Mission* (Tamiris / music, Pitot and radio text, David Greggory): The Committee with Sydne Becker and Bettina Harris as New England, Vivian Cherry and Judy Jaffe as The Middle West, Ida Soyer as The South, Tamiris as California, Maurice Silvers as Man with Radio and Daniel Nagrin as Voice of the Radio

Piano, Genevieve Pitot; singers for *Liberty Song* Mimi Bensell and Leon Lishchiner and for *Negro Spirituals* Laura Duncan, Bob Moman and Dora Thompson; costumes for *Liberty Song*, Rhoda Rammelkamp, for *Negro Spirituals*, Liz Reitell and for *Good-Will Mission*, Norma Fuller; percussions for *Liberty Song*, Jack Wolf; decor for *Good-Will Mission*, Grant Code

Tamiris' Studio Theatre, 1940-1944

Medical Aid to Russia Benefit

Helen Tamiris and her Dance Group

Feb 7 1942   eve   Great Neck, Long Island: Chapel Theatre

Liberty Song: What a Court Hath Old England Tamiris with Sydne Becker, Bettina Harris, Ida Soyer, Maurice Silvers, Gilda Bronze and Judy Jaffe, *My Days Have Been So Wondrous Free* Tamiris and Daniel Nagrin, *Bunker Hill* Tamiris with Bettina Harris, Ida Soyer and Daniel Nagrin and *Ode to the Fourth of July* Tamiris with Sydne Becker, Gilda Bronze, Bettina Harris, Judy Jaffee, Ida Soyer and Daniel Nagrin; *Negro Spirituals:* [*Wade in the Water* Bettina Harris, Ida Little and Ida Soyer,] *Go Down Moses* Tamiris, [*Ezekiel Saw de Wheel* Ida Soyer, *It's Me, It's Me, Oh Lord* Ida Little,] *Swing Low, Sweet Chariot* Tamiris, *Git on Board Lil Chillen* Tamiris, *Joshua Fit de Battle ob Jericho* Tamiris, *Crucifixion* Tamiris and *When the Saints Go Marchin' In* Tamiris with Sydne Becker, Bettina Harris, Ida Little and Ida Soyer; *Good-Will Mission* The Committee with Sydne Becker and Bettina Harris as Boston, Mass, Vivian Cherry and Judy Jaffee as The Middle West, Ida Soyer as The South, Tamiris as California, Maurice Silvers as Man with Radio and Daniel Nagrin as Voice of the Radio

Piano, Genevieve Pitot

Students' Dance Recitals, Washington Irving High School

Helen Tamiris and her Group

Mar 7 1942   eve   New York: Memorial Auditorium

Liberty Song: What a Court Hath Old England Tamiris with Sydne Becker, Bettina Harris, Ida Soyer, Maurice Silvers, Gilda Bronze and Judy Jaffee, *My Days Have Been So Wondrous Free* Tamiris and Daniel Nagrin, *Bunker Hill* Tamiris with Bettina Harris, Ida Soyer and Daniel Nagrin and *Ode to the Fourth of July* Tamiris with Sydne Becker, Gilda Bronze, Bettina Harris, Judy Jaffee, Ida Soyer and Daniel Nagrin; *Negro Spirituals:* [*Wade in the Water* Bettina Harris, Ida Little and Ida Soyer,] *Go Down Moses* Tamiris, *It's Me, It's Me, Oh Lord* Ida Little, *Swing Low, Sweet Chariot* Tamiris, *Git on Board Lil Chillen* Tamiris, [*Ezekiel Saw de Wheel* Ida Soyer,] *Joshua Fit de Battle ob Jericho* Tamiris, *Crucifixion* Tamiris and *When the Saints Go Marchin' In* Tamiris with Sydne Becker, Bettina Harris, Ida Little and Ida Soyer; *Good-Will Mission:* The Committee with Sydne Becker and Bettina Harris as Boston Mass, Judy Jaffee as The Middle West, Ida Soyer as The South, Tamiris as California, Maurice Silvers as Man with Radio and Arthur Elmer as Voice of the Radio

Piano, Genevieve Pitot; singers for *Liberty Song*, Mimi Benzell and Leon Lischener

First Rainbow Room Appearance

Helen Tamiris, assisted by Ida Soyer and Daniel Nagrin

Apr 1 1942 (Opening date of six weeks engagement)   eves   New York: Rockefeller Center

[Leo Reisman and his Orchestra; The Comedy Star Billy de Wolfe;] The Distinguished Dancer Helen Tamiris assisted by Ida Soyer and Daniel Nagrin in "American Themes": *Negro Spirituals*[62] Tamiris, *Waterfront Serenade* (Tamiris / Pitot) Tamiris and Daniel

---

[62] There is evidence that the *Negro Spirituals* performed were *Little David, Play on Your Harp, Joshua Fit de Battle ob Jericho, Ezekial Saw the Wheel, Go Down Moses, When the*

Rainbow Room Appearance, cont
Nagrin and *My Days Have Been So Wondrous Free* from *Liberty Song* Tamiris and Daniel Nagrin with vocal accompaniment by Mimi Benzelle and Leon Lischener, Musical Director and Pianist Genevieve Pitot; [The Song Favorite Eleanor French; Clemente and his Rumba Band featuring Dacita]

Second Rainbow Room Appearance

Helen Tamiris, assisted by Ida Soyer and Milton Feher

Oct 28 1942 (Opening date of six weeks engagement)   eves   New York: Rockefeller Center

[Leo Reisman and his Orchestra; Leonard Elliott, comedian, with Irma Jruist, piano; Victoria Cordova, Latin Songstress; Dacita and her Rhumba Sextet, Dr Sidney Ross, magician;] The Distinguished Dancer Helen Tamiris assisted by Ida Soyer and Milton Feher in *Bayou Ballads: Suzette* Tamiris and Feher, *When Your Potatoe's Done* Soyer and Feher, *Pity Poor Mlle Zizi* Tamiris with Soyer and Feher and *Little Carnival* Tamiris with Soyer and Feher; *Go Down Moses* Tamiris

Choreography, Tamiris; music arranged from *Negro Songs of Louisiana* by Ernest Lubin; piano, Paul Creston; singers, Emile Renan and Rosa Akerston

Students' Dance Recitals, Washington Irving High School

Helen Tamiris, assisted by Ida Soyer, Milton Feher and Bettina Harris

Feb 27 1943   eve   New York: Central H S of Needle Trades

[*For the Tired Business Man*] *Diversion* from *Momentum*; [*War Face* (Soyer / Berenice Stone) Ida Soyer;] [*Themes of 1940*] *Song of Today* Tamiris; Piano solo, Paul Creston; *Impressions of the Bull Ring* Tamiris; [*The Last Spring* (Soyer / Berenice Stone) Soyer]; *Ode to Stalingrad* (Tamiris / Ernest Lubin and Paul Creston) Tamiris; *My Days Have Been So Wondrous Free* from *Liberty Song* Tamiris and Milton Feher; *Bayou Ballads: Suzette* Tamiris with Milton Feher, *When Your Potatoe's Done* Ida Soyer and Milton Feher, *Pity Poor Mlle Zizi* Tamiris with Ida Soyer and Milton Feher and *Little Carnival* Tamiris with Ida Soyer and Milton Feher; *Negro Spirituals: Little David* (Tamiris / arr Pitot) Tamiris with Ida Soyer and Bettina Harris, [*Ezekiel Saw de Wheel* (Soyer / arr Pitot) Ida Soyer,] *Go Down Moses* Tamiris, [*It's Me, It's Me, O Lord* (Little / arr Pitot) Bettina Harris,] *Crucifixion* Tamiris and *When the Saints Go Marchin' In* Tamiris with Ida Soyer and Bettina Harris

Piano, Paul Creston; singers, Rose Akerston and Emile Renan; tympani, Robert Wolf; trumpet, Leona May Smith

It's Up to You

Apr 11 1943 (Opening)   Washington D.C.: Skouras Theatre

Performed as Prologue in motion picture theatres
Producers: Skouras Theatres, The American Theatre Wing and the Food Industries in cooperation with the U.S. Department of Agriculture; book, Aurthur Arent; music, Earl Robinson; lyrics, Lewis Allan, Alfred Hayes

---

Saints Go Marching In, No Hidin' Place, Swing Low, Sweet Chariot and *Get on Board Lil Chillen.*

Tamiris' Studio Theatre, 1940-1944

and Hi Zaret; projections, Howard Bay; lighting, Moe Hack; costumes, Peggy Clark; direction, Elia Kazan

Scenes

Dig, Farmer, Dig! "It's Up to You" sung by Earl Robinson and Jack de Merchant with quartette James Dobson, Richard C. Hart, Guy Spaul and Oliver Thorndike; *Rationing* "Get the Point, Mrs Brown?" sung by Richard Beckhard, Louisa Horton, Louise Larabee, Dulcie Cooper, Anna Minot and Laura Duncan; *Plain Men in Dirty Overalls* "Plain Men in Dirty Overalls" written and sung by Earl Robinson; *Black Market* "Porterhouse Lucy" sung by John Huntington with quartette Lester Lonergan, Farrell Pell, Percy Helton and Wendell Corey; *Porterhouse Lucy*[63] danced by Helen Tamiris assisted by Oliver Thorndyke, Edward Nannery, David Tyrell and Walter Palm; *We Can Take It* "We Can Take It" sung by Laura Duncan; *Waste!* "Victory Begins at Home" sung by Jack de Merchant, Laura Duncan and company.

Students' Dance Recitals, Central High School of Needle Trades

Helen Tamiris

Mar 5 1944[64]   New York: Needle Trades HS Auditorium

Liberty Song: What a Court Hath Old England Muriel Brenner, Aldo Cadena, Margaret Cuddy, Lidija Franklin, Olga Lunick, Daniel Nagrin, Clara Nezin, Kathleen O'Brien and Emy St Just, *My Days Have Been So Wondrous Free* Tamiris and Daniel Nagrin, *Bunker Hill* Emy St Just, Aldo Cadena, Olga Lunick, Clara Nezin, Daniel Nagrin and Paul Sweeney and *Ode to the Fourth of July* Tamiris with Muriel Brenner, Aldo Cadena, Margaret Cuddy, Lidija Franklin, Olga Lunick, Daniel Nagrin, Clara Nezin, Kathleen O'Brien, Paul Sweeney and Emy St Just; *Spanish Dance* (Tamiris and Nagrin / Albeniz-Pitot) Tamiris and Daniel Nagrin; *Ode to Stalingrad* Tamiris; *Bayou Ballads: Suzette* Tamiris and Daniel Nagrin, *When Your Potatoes' Done* Kathleen O'Brien and Daniel Nagrin, *Pity Poor Mlle Zizi* Tamiris and Daniel Nagrin and *Little Carnival* Tamiris with Emy St Just and Daniel Nagrin; *John Brown* (Nagrin / Pitot) Daniel Nagrin; *Negro Spirituals: Little David Play on Your Harp* Muriel Brenner, Margaret Cuddy and Emy St Just, *Go Down Moses* Tamiris, *No Hidin' Place* Daniel Nagrin, *Crucifixion* Tamiris and *When the Saints Go Marchin' In* Tamiris with Muriel Brenner, Margaret Cuddy, Daniel Nagrin, Kathleen O'Brien and Emy St Just

Musical Direction and piano, Genevieve Pitot; singers, Rosa Akerston and Emil Renan; tympani, David Ginsburg; trumpet, John V. Pinto; lighting, Howard Corderey; costumes: for *Liberty Song*, Rhoda Rammelkamp, for *Bayou Ballads*, *Ode to Stalingrad*, *Spanish Dance* and *Negro Spirituals*, Tamiris and for *John Brown*, Nagrin

The People's Bandwagon

Sept 26 1944 (Opening?)   Boston: Symphony Hall   25-city tour

Helen Tamiris and Daniel Nagrin, dancers; Mary Lou Williams, pianist; Orelia and Pedro, Latin-American dancers; Will Geer, Lincolnian actor; Woody Guthrie, folk singer[65]

---

[63] Choreography, Tamiris. *Life* wrote up the *Porterhouse Lucy* scene with pictures of Tamiris. Part of the lyrics quoted included the following:
> Temptation looks around to see if Uncle Sam's eagle
> Is watching, then whispers, "Porterhouse? Ain't you illegal?"
> "Illegal, Ilshmegal," says Porterhouse Lucy,
> The point is I'm rare and I'm thick and I'm juicy!"
> Vol 14, No 17 (Apr 26 1943) p 28

[64] There is evidence that Tamiris appeared in this same series on March 11 1945, but no program is available.

[65] This information is taken from Tamiris' notes. More complete information is unavailable.

6 MISS TAMIRIS ON BROADWAY, 1944–1955

WHEN HELEN TAMIRIS decided that she wished to continue speaking to the multitudes—as in Federal Theatre—rather than to the few—as on concert stages, she found dance just beginning to come of age on Broadway. Musical comedy, the genre which used it for the multitudes, had, despite its title, depended solely on dialogue to advance its plots. Music and especially dancing were subsidiary to the story presented, subsidiary to the point of being unrelated. A good song or, even more, an exciting dance was thrown in for diversion, for entertainment, for fun. Until *Oklahoma!* of 1943. Dancing in it was used for the first time for an intrinsic reason rather than for interpolated fun. Its dancing contributed to character development and added dramatic atmosphere. A decade and a half later, in *West Side Story,* dancing had achieved such importance that *it* advanced the plot, with music and dialogue growing out of physical action on the stage. Agnes de Mille with her dream ballet in *Oklahoma!* and Jerome Robbins with his *ballet d'action* called *West Side Story* demark the beginning and the culmination of the success story of dance on Broadway. Dance had come into its own by being able to say something to an audience—to tell stories, to express emotions, to diffuse atmosphere.

"Isn't it remarkable, Miss Tamiris, how the dance has caught on practically overnight?" someone gushed to Tamiris at one time during these years.

"Yes, it is remarkable," she said she answered, "but it's been a long night."

For the kind of dance that had caught on seemingly overnight was the kind of dance the moderns had been championing a decade before that—on another planet called the "concert field" about a step away from Broadway. It was the kind of dance that insisted that something more than physical tricks or flashy display was inherent in movement. It was the kind of dance that insisted that dancing was before an audience to provide something more than just fun. It was modern dance that had become a meaningful element in musical comedy and in turn took over Broadway as no other kind of dance had done. By means of modern dance, dance became equal to music and dialogue in one of the major divisions of the Broadway theatre, the musical comedy.

If Agnes de Mille accomplished the breakthrough and Jerome Robbins is remembered for the achievement, Helen Tamiris is one of those who solidified and advanced the gain. In between the two demarking dates, 1943 and 1957, she choreographed eighteen musical comedies, fourteen of which had runs on Broadway, six of which were long runs, among them the famous *Up in Central Park* of 1945 (remembered for its Currier and Ives skating ballet), *Annie Get Your Gun* of 1946 (remembered for its Indian Dance featuring Daniel Nagrin—as well as Ethel Merman), *Inside U.S.A.* (headlined for its *Tiger Lily* and *Haunted House* ballet d'actions featuring Valerie Bettis—as well as Beatrice Lillie), *By the Beautiful Sea* of 1954 (remembered for its underwater ballet—as well as for Ezio Pinza), and *Plain and Fancy* of 1955 (evoked for its tender *By Lantern Light* dance featuring Daniel Nagrin). Few choreographers—only Hanya Holm and Agnes de Mille of the same generation—can compare with this record in either quantity or quality.

No small part of Tamiris' success during these years was her liking for and ability to work with people. She wrote, "In all collaborations, the technique for survival exists through the process of give and take, in proper amounts. I have found," she continued, "after years of trial and error in the Broadway theatre, what with not giving and taking either too much or too little, that with the maximum amount of perseverance and some muscle power, creative collaboration can be one of the most rewarding experiences in life." "Creative collaboration"—here is the existential Tamiris seizing the moment of contact with others and finding it life-fulfilling. There was no thought of collaboration as compromise; rather it was creative, self-enriching, productive.

This point of view was evident in two aspects of her work on Broadway: first in her relationship with her dancers and second in her relationship with her co-directors.

As she had never developed a technique back in the thirties when she was working with "Her Group" but rather made suggestions and brought out reactions from her dancers, so now with her dancers in the corps she expected each individual to assume the responsibility of individual expression. Thus she was unable to work with a ballet dancer whose training was based on the traditional *danse d'ecole;* she demanded movement that grew out of the immediate necessity.

In an interview with E. C. Sherburn of the *Christian Science Monitor,* Miss Tamiris told how she derived the movements and put together the choreography for *Up in Central Park*'s skating ballet. First she discerned the specific truth of every skating movement she wished to use, the determining factor being the special character that a skate on ice gives to movement. Then the dancers themselves were required, with their instinct for expression, to contribute "notes of color unique to them, to the enlivenment of the total effect." Out of this process sprang a group of phrases; fresh dance, true to its theme, resulted. Always, she said, she asked herself in her work, "What is the specific detail that gives character to a movement? The answer to that question must be found and respected. If the truthful cause of a movement is adhered to, the result will be truthfully and individually expressive, as well as a manifestation of technical accomplishment."

This was simple in theory, but it had taken her years to achieve. Even yet she had to instill in her dancers the understanding of how important each was to the whole. "The individual performing must see his part in the whole," she insisted, "for the whole can succeed only when the parts succeed, for all parts have a responsibility to each other." No Tamiris dancer carried her stamp; each was himself in the whole.

Her job then became that of putting the parts together so that they achieved the effect of a beginning, middle, and end, were as integrated as a part of a story or a play to a whole. The dance gained form out of its own substance. What could be more "modern" than this process? Obviously, this theory of form growing out of use, out of its own organism, made Tamiris a member of all the moderns in all the arts, no matter what the medium. Her emphasis on the uniqueness of each dancer in that organism and of his own "notes of color" was pure Tamiris. Its being ephemeral did not vitiate its effect on the dancers who worked with her.

A list of the dancers whom she gave opportunity to color her stages is full of the next generation of modern dancers: Daniel Nagrin and Valerie Bettis achieved the most spectacular success under her tutelage. Others included Mary Anthony, Dorothy Bird, Pearl Lang and Pearl Primus, Talley Beatty, Donald McKayle, Bertram Ross and David Wood, Bambi Linn and Rod Alexander—the programs below provide any number of other names. Much mention in the newspapers was made of the fact that Miss Tamiris' dancing corps were mixed racially. In *Show Boat* there was reason inherent in the script to have two groups of dancers—one colored (what we now call black) and one white, but the dances in the revue *Inside U. S. A.* had mixed corps for no obvious reason except that each chosen was an excellent dancer no matter what his color. Long before it became fashionable, Miss Tamiris lived integration. Such practice was another example of her greatness as a human being.

Her collaboration with her producers and co-directors was similarly "creative." For example, the producer for the revue *Inside U. S. A.*, Arthur Schwartz, came to Tamiris with his overall plan. He said that so far ten songs needed ideas for staging: some needed out-and-out choreography while others needed just staging for singers. Also, the first act needed a production number—or a "ballet," he said off-handedly—for a song called *Haunted Heart*, and an idea was needed for a "ballet" for the second act. Miss Tamiris seized her opportunities with gusto. For *Haunted Heart* she devised a *ballet d'action*, with comic strip overtones, for the enchanting Valerie Bettis to tell the story of the song in movement while John Tyers sang the words. Then, in keeping with the theme of the production suggested by the Gunther book, Miss Tamiris picked up the American newspapers' penchant for glamorizing murder, in her second act assignment. The resultant *Tiger Lily*, danced again by Bettis, with a large chorus, satirized this practice by treating murder as a circus, in unmistakable movements that told the story without words and at the same time commented on this American dementia.

In giving Miss Tamiris this assignment, Schwartz knew that she would contribute to the whole already laid out. He knew that she knew that choreography in revues as well as musical comedies should at its best grow out of the scripts. He knew that she practiced the craft of letting the script determine the style and content of the numbers she would devise. For, as she wrote, "I maintain that the choreographer is at the mercy of the script, just so, because if the script is not the determining factor, of content, of style, in fact every detail of the dances, the unity of the show is destroyed. Sometimes," she continued, "a choreographer is lucky when the book gives him room to expand and at other times he is lucky if he gets even one spot that calls attention to his work as such. An arrogant choreographer," she admitted, "will force his own conception beyond the limits of the script and in this manner may get rave notices for his dances while throwing the show completely out of balance. . . ."

"On the other hand," she wrote for the benefit of her co-workers in the other arts, "I think too few writers really understand how much the dance can speak for them, that it can sometimes carry a plot forward with more intensity and theatricality and, in its proper place, be more eloquent than speech. Just as the choreographer must respect and not abuse the script, so also must the authors not degrade the dance by using it as an inane relaxing interlude in the progress of the story."

In reviewing *Park Avenue*, Miss Tamiris' seventh musical and her fourth success on Broadway, John Martin revealed that the choreographer practiced what she preached, and at the same time pointed a lesson for all choreographers: "All she does," he wrote with tongue-in-cheek, "is steep herself in the style, the dramatic and musical content, the theatrical method, of the material she is working on and evolve movement to heighten them where they need heightening. Of course, . . . nothing is required except talent, sensitivity and ability to see a show whole."

The acute Martin also pointed out that, in order to see Miss Tamiris' real genius, the big production numbers like *Tiger Lily* were not the only aspects to be considered. "Also and chiefly, one should be aware of the countless little phrases that illumine the action, the mood, the wit, of a song or an ensemble. For example," he elucidated, "in the opening of *Park Avenue*, the piquant Dorothy Bird has her back to the house as the curtain opens. She is rehearsing for a wedding. Instantly the audience is made aware of the lightly satirical flavor of the work as a whole, the drawing-room dimensions of its actions, its literate wit." Often such a touch is so light, people are not even aware it is dancing at all. "It is dancing nonetheless and supplies all the theatrical quality there is in a piece that is primarily talk."

Martin's evaluation of Miss Tamiris' ability already in evidence this early in her career on Broadway is interesting. Miss Tamiris' ability to see a show whole is rare, he made clear again:

> She has no sense of using a show merely as a means for exploitation of the show. Her movement is always, within the limits of the medium, expressive, inherent in the immediate content of the action, and, again within the limitations of the medium, creative. She shows few if any displays of virtuosity as such, and no effort whatever to stop the show. Indeed quite the reverse: the effort is to keep the show going.
>
> Musical comedy is a composite, and none of its elements—music, drama, dance, decor—can come into the synthesis in pure form. To adapt them, however, to the necessities of a total theatrical situation is not to compromise them in any way, for the truly theatrically minded artist will not even be tempted to look down his nose at such limitations.

Miss Tamiris was not the first choreographer to see the possibilities of the medium, Martin admitted. "Nevertheless," he summed up, "it would be difficult to point out another choreographer who has so consciously, so consistently and so adroitly made it her basis of action. By carrying over the tenets of the modern dance, she has introduced into the musical a wonderfully frank and honest expressiveness that is quite novel."

After an apprenticeship period in doing choreography quickly for the summer resorts of trade unions, Miss Tamiris choreographed dances for her first musical play, *Marianne,* in late 1943. Opening in Washington, D. C. in January 1944, it quietly closed. *Stovepipe Hat,* another musical play, based on the Lincoln legend, had some strong dances, especially one at a White House levee, but it too closed, in Boston. Next, Miss Tamiris was part of the revue *The People's Bandwagon,* during the 1944 re-election campaign of President Roosevelt, but this was only an interim job. Success on Broadway was what she was after.

Miss Tamiris' jinx for closing on the road was broken with the Michael Todd Production of *Up in Central Park* in 1945. Its success included a long run, a road company production, and a movie.[66] Its choreography, revealing an amused attitude that neither ridiculed nor condescended to its late-nineteenth-century period, was perfect for this popular Sigmund Romberg musical. In the opening of the scene, the audience saw tableaus of Currier and Ives prints that were like cameos. Then, accompanied by the lilting "May I Show You My Currier and Ives?" song, the static scene became alive when the backdrop of the lounge of the Stetson Hotel set rose and disclosed a snow-covered landscape with flakes falling on the dancers—who began to move. This was the famous skating ballet never equalled by any ballet company.[67] There were also dances in the scenes called *Rip Van Winkle, The Fireman's Bride,* and *Maypole Dance*—all excellent, said *Variety* which labeled *Up in Central Park* one of the finest operettas in a decade.

Pearl Primus was her leading dancer in Miss Tamiris' next choreography for a revival of the 1920s *Show Boat.* Primus was Sal who danced *No Shoes* with Laverne French as Sam, and she was the Dahomey Queen in *Dance of the Dahomeys* and *Avenue A Release* with Alma Sutton, Claude Marchant, and Talley Beatty. Two dancing choruses (the white and the black) added to the success of this perennial favorite revived by Jerome Kern and Oscar Hammerstein 2nd in 1946. There was a touring company following the Broadway closing after 418 performances, and City Center produced it again in 1948 with Miss Tamiris re-staging her old dances.

Daniel Nagrin had not only danced as a lead in *Up in Central Park*

[66] Movies always intrigued Tamiris as another means to reach the masses with her dance. However, except for this movie of *Up in Central Park* for which she re-set the choreography, and a movie called *Just for You,* made in 1952 and featuring Daniel Nagrin, Tamiris refused to work in Hollywood. She found the intervention of the director, the cameraman, and the cutter too determining to her dances before they reached the masses.
[67] Frederick Ashton revived his 1937 *Les Patineurs* for Ballet Theatre in October of 1946. It was reviewed as singularly static in comparison with Miss Tamiris' recent dance on the same theme.

but he had also assisted Miss Tamiris in her choreography for all of her productions so far. In her next show, he became a star as "The Wild Horse" in *Wild Horse Ceremonial Dance,* the central scene in *Annie Get Your Gun.* It was an eye-filling production number as the Indian braves quivered, vibrated, and stomped, but true to her theory of not letting a dance run away with a show, Miss Tamiris soon brought into the middle of the scene the Annie of the title, danced by Ethel Merman on Broadway and Mary Martin on the road. A dance striking in its own right in actuality served to advance the plot. By the time of the production, 1946, Miss Tamiris was ranked with director Joshua Logan and designer Jo Mielziner as "leaders in their fields" and "the kind of people the producers insist on having around."

The less successful *Park Avenue* had just the right touch of light satire in its dancing despite the fact that the choreography had been started by Eugene Loring and re-done by Miss Tamiris on the road. Dorothy Bird (who with Nagrin assisted on the choreography) was lauded for her effectiveness in the scene *Sweet Nevada* (the dance was titled *In the Courtroom* and had a large cast which included dancers William Skipper, Harold Mattox, and Joan Mann), although the musical as a whole was found to be a boring and distasteful joke about divorce.

Miss Tamiris herself was very excited about her opportunity of being associate director of the 1947 *The Great Campaign,* a production put on by the Experimental Theatre. With the author of the book, Arnold Sundgaard, who wrote both this and the following *The Promised Valley,* Miss Tamiris found great rapport. "He tries to think of music and dance as part of the vocabulary of speech," she wrote of her association with Sundgaard. "He too, feels that when words are no longer capable of communication that music and movement are legitimate means of expressing ideas and emotions." As an experimental production, *The Great Campaign* ran for only five performances; *The Promised Valley,* produced during that same summer in Salt Lake City, for the state's centennial, reached many more people and was far more elaborate. Working with it, Tamiris felt her old sense of mission as she brought excellent modern dance to the provinces and found it understood and appreciated. Her work there with Virginia Tanner perhaps supplied the impetus which has led to the recent development of a Dance Repertory Company there.

But Miss Tamiris left her pioneering efforts for modern dance in inner America and returned to Broadway to choreograph and stage numbers for her most spectacular success, *Inside U. S. A.* Its revue form allowed great latitude for her imagination and she let it go so that, as Walter Terry pointed out, all dancers had a feeling of smugness when, at the opening performance, with a star great and famous, a production lavish, the skits hilarious, yet a dancer was able to stop the show twice and generate rave reviews. This was Valerie Bettis in her two *ballets d'action* by Tamiris—*Haunted Heart* and *Tiger Lily.* The dancer and her partner Eric Victor received the first annual award of the "Show of the Month Club," a plaque for their "distinguished creative and artistic performance on the American Musical Stage."

Besides these two numbers, Tamiris staged the other scenes, providing short, frequent, and appropriate dance interludes in the skits *Blue Grass, First Prize at the Fair, At the Mardi Gras,* and *My Gal is Mine Once More.* "Through dance actions," Terry wrote, "Tamiris gives body-response to the rhythms of the music, reflected the pictures suggested by the lyrics, and established the prevailing moods of the scenes." Despite the fact that *Playbill* was now lamenting the influence of modern dance in abolishing the "line-up" on Broadway—"I wonder if there's any chorus any more that could do an over-the-top or even an off-to-Buffalo"—*Inside U. S. A.* gave a healthy boost to dance when it needed it.

During the next five years, Miss Tamiris choreographed or staged and choreographed seven musicals on Broadway. The revue form of *Touch and Go* of 1949 allowed her two *ballets d'action* with Daniel Nagrin and Pearl Lang: *American Primitive* combining sharp and gauche patterns with the bounce and joy of country dance, and *Under the Sleeping Volcano* using tense dynamics from the Latin temperament (Ilona Murrai was another dancer featured in the latter). *Broadway Love Song* was a duet for Pearl Lang as a forlorn and hopeless young lady who has failed on Broadway and Jonathan Lucas as an adoring bellhop. All three dances showed Miss Tamiris at her best in using the modern dance idiom on Broadway. *Great to Be Alive* suffered from a turgid script but shone with the sultry dancing and Bankheadian voice of Valerie Bettis. In the major number *Dreams Ago*, Bambi Linn and Rod Alexander waltzed as lovers long dead, against which number was juxtaposed *The Story of Kitty*, a both vulgar and elegant recounting of the life of a continental siren danced by Valerie Bettis assisted by David Nillo. Mention should also be made of the opening number in which Miss Tamiris introduced the audience to the members of the ghost world who populated the play and caused the complications. It was another example of the choreographer's instinctive integration of dance action with acting, speech, song, and stage pictorialism. Its title also was apropos—and charming: *When the Sheets Come Home from the Laundry.*

Bless You All, Flahooley, and *Carnival in Flanders* fared from well to badly. In the first, Valerie Bettis did what *Time* called "a belly dance in Morocco." Actually it was a tongue-in-cheek take-off on sultry *ballets d'action* that only a Tamiris would do on her own ballets such as *Tiger Lily. Flahooley* starred Yma Sumac, now forgotten—the singer whose voice spread four octaves. More remembered are the Bil Baird Marionettes which were also featured. *Carnival in Flanders* closed after only six performances.

By the Beautiful Sea had the asset of Shirley Booth to carry an otherwise limited show. Called in after the show was in rehearsal, Miss Tamiris put several numbers in shape in two weeks with her now legendary craftsmanship and nimble theatricality. Under her doctoring and with the help of Nagrin, the *Spicy Pictures* dance became broad but funny, and the *Throw That Anchor Away* lusty but pitched right. *Fanny* also had a star to carry it—Ezio Pinza, and, as in *By the Beautiful Sea*, spectacular sets and lighting by Jo Mielziner gave delight even if the book was weak. An underwater ballet behind fish net and a circus dance were Tamiris' contribution to another made-over production.

If *Annie Get Your Gun* was Miss Tamiris' most successful musical and *Inside U. S. A.* her most spectacular, *Plain and Fancy* was her most sensitive. For it, her last, she staged the musical numbers as well as choreographed the dances, a chore she had enjoyed many times during her fat decade of successes. Three make-overs recently behind her, now she wanted and got a show in which she was involved from its inception; now she wanted and got a show in which she was allowed completely to be creative in the entire collaboration.

Plain and Fancy was about the Pennsylvania folk, the Amish, who, of all things for a musical comedy, eschewed dancing and repressed romance. Instinctively, the sensitive Miss Tamiris found the essence of these simple-complex people in something like warm gaucheness and a shy romanticism. And these were attributes, she knew, that could best be revealed, not through witty words or public songs, but through subtle movements. The states she sought to express were too deep for verbalization in word or song; these were feelings best expressed in movement. Modern dance always claimed to be able to express inner states; could it express the essence of the Amish?

The resounding answer to Miss Tamiris' questing was the sensitive staging and choreography she devised for *Plain and Fancy*. All was subtly done and theatrically right. Especially touching was the one dance *By Lantern Light*, with Nagrin as Samuel Zook, in which the Amish code was accepted affectionately and the Amish feelings were portrayed lovingly. True empathy with these people permeated the very texture of the dance. Also, *This Is All Very New to Me* was staged delightfully as the singers and dancers sang and moved and were interrupted periodically and logically by others. Wit, vitality, character—all were intrinsic to the scene. The striking *How Do You Raise a Barn?*, with its rhythmical and lyrical building of a barn on stage, invariably brought excitement to and applause from the audience; the spectacular carnival scene, with Nagrin now as fiery Mambo Joe, served as vivid contrast to the rest of the Pennsylvania farm setting. (Walter Terry reported that "Nagrin's swift, physically virtuosic, dramatically insinuating actions found stunning outlet in Miss Tamiris' choreography.") *Plain and Fancy* was a fitting denouement for Miss Tamiris on Broadway—a simple theme simply expressed—so subtly.[68]

"In the early days, in the Twenties," she wrote in 1948, "there were many times when I doubted that modern dance would ever reach a large audience. But the years of the Great Depression and the experience of working as a choreographer for the Federal Theatre Project settled that doubt. When Charles Weidman's *Candide* and my *How Long, Brethren?* and *Adelante* were presented to cheering audiences

---

[68] Of Tamiris' last dances, *Memoir* (Tamiris / Carlos Chavez) and *Women's Song* (Tamiris / Norman Dello Joio) were her most important. She had returned to the concert stage with a company of herself as artistic director and Daniel Nagrin, her husband. She died on August 5 1966 at the age of 64.

that had never seen a dance recital, I knew that the modern dance was not an esoteric passing phase of dance to be enjoyed only by the cognoscenti, but one that could reach large audiences." The few surviving records (mere glimpses) of her movement that was the basis of her appeal to the masses—the movement that was Tamiris—are four *Negro Spirituals* filmed by the William Skipper Corporation in 1959.

There is still doubt in this historian's mind as to the ultimate fate of modern dance, still only a third of a century old in 1972. In this art there have been, as this chronicle has shown—and are—too few Tamirises who wish to speak to large audiences; most are content to be enjoyed only by their kind of cognoscenti. Any swerving from solitary single-minded pursuit of individual goals is anathema. Cooperation is compromise; creative collaboration in the living moment for the benefit of a large audience is a Tamiris legacy largely ignored.

What has not been ignored? Certainly she helped the Negro dancer toward acceptance. From the broad point of view, this resulted, logically, from her sense of mission. But even more, one can see that her greatest legacy was her affirmation of all of life, than which, as John Martin wrote, there is nothing more social. Young modern choreographers today carry on with her courage and mission when they face the dynamic actualities of a new present—and react simply and straightforwardly. Some call these "Avant garde" crude, vulgar, obscene; they are charged with working without form; they seem to care only for the moment by producing works that, by intention, live once and are gone. The attacks are familiar when one surveys the artistic life of a Tamiris. She too received such criticism as she felt—lived—a dance that recognized—affirmed—life in all its aspects in her alive now. Her "lust for movement" embarrassed many. But her existential approach to her art required that "lust" be recognized, that "movement" should ever change, that "now" was art's *raison d'être*. This is the Tamiris legacy— keeping modern dance modern in that essence of modernity: a responsiveness to the unformulated will of an epoch, a drive to do what a time requires.

Marianne

History: Opened Jan 10 1944 (?) Washington D.C.: National Theatre   Closed on the road

Production details: production, B. P. Schulberg and Marion Gering; book, Sylvia Regan and Kenneth White; music, Abraham Ellstein; lyrics, Beatrice and Lothar Metzl and Robert B. Sour; choreography, Helen Tamiris; settings, Frederick Fox; costumes, Ken Barr

Musical Program: *What Do I Have to Do* Mary Jane Walsh as Suzanne and Val Valentinoff as Francois; *Kind of a Man* Virginia MacWatters as Martine and Jerry Wayne as Toni; *Vive Pichon* company; *Marianne* Mary Jane Walsh as Suzanne; *Always Goodbye* Jerry Wayne as Toni and Virginia MacWatters as Martine; *Crepe Suzette* Mary Jane Walsh as Suzanne; *No More* Virginia MacWatters as Martine; *The Germ in the German* Harold Patrick as Dr. Dubois and Jean Darling and Marjorie Hayward as villagers; *Out of the Dark* Jerry Wayne as Toni; *The Pom Pom on Your Hat* Mary Jane Walsh as Suzanne and Val Valentinoff as Francois; *My Heart Is Like a Bird* Virginia MacWatters as Martine; *The Black Horsemen* company

Assistant to Tamiris, Daniel Nagrin; piano for Tamiris, Charles Magnan

Dancers: Dorothy Bird, Kathleen O'Brien, Charles Bockman, Vivian Cherry, Clara Cordery, Lidija Franklin, Joseph Gifford, Miriam Kornfield, Olga Lunich, Daniel Nagrin, Hazel Roy, Emy St Just, Ida Soyer, Jack Star and Barbara Bray

Stovepipe Hat

History: Opened May 18 1944 (4 performances)   New Haven: Shubert Theatre   Moved May 23 1944   Boston: Shubert Theatre   Closed May 27 1944[69]

Production details: production, Carl E. Ring; book and lyrics, Walter F. Hannan, Edward Heyman and Harold Spina; music, Harold Spina; staging, Robert Ross; choreography, Helen Tamiris; settings and costumes, Lucinda Ballard and A. A. Ostrander

Musical Program: unavailable

Partial cast list: Bob Kennedy, Frederic Tozere, Ann Warren, Parker Fennelly, Joan Chandler, Duval Springman, John Garth 3rd, Joy Geffin, Ruth White, Morton L. Stevens, Madeleine Clive, Jimmie Elliott, Paul Ransom, Morton De Costa and Dorothy Johnson

Others: Richard A. Gordon Choir; Eva Jessye Choir; Helen Tamiris dancers Daniel Nagrin, Lidija Franklin, Joseph Franklin, Mary Anthony, George Bockman, Emy St Just and Lavinia Niehaust (Nielsen?)

Up in Central Park

Broadway history: Opened Jan 27 1945   New York: New Century Theatre   Closed Apr 13 1946 after 504 performances

Production details: production, Michael Todd; book, Herbert and Dorothy Fields; lyrics, Dorothy Field; music, Sigmund Romberg; book staging, John Kennedy; dances, Helen Tamiris; settings and lighting, Howard Bay; costumes, Grace Houston and Ernest Schraps

Musical Program: *Up from the Gutter* Betty Bruce as Bessie, Maureen Cannon as Rosie, Walter Burke as Danny, Charles Irwin as Timothy with singers and dancers; *Carrousel in the Park* Maureen Cannon as Rosie; *It Doesn't Cost You Anything to Dream* Maureen Cannon as Rosie, Betty Bruce as Bessie and Wilbur Evans as John; *Boss Tweed* Noah Berry as Tweed, Rowan Tudor as Oakey Hall, George Lance as Connolly, Harry Meehan as Sweeney, James McElhoney as Monroe, Paul Reed as Peters, Charles Irwin as Timothy and men; *Opening* singing girls and boys; *When She Walks in the Room* Wilbur Evans as John; *Currier and Ives* Betty Bruce as Bessie and Fred Barry as Joe with Daniel Nagrin as Daniel with dancers [*The Skating Ballet*]; *Close as Pages in a Book* Maureen Cannon as Rosie and Wilbur Evans as John; *Rip Van Winkle* Maureen Cannon as Rosie, Betty Bruce as Bessie, Noah Berry as Tweed, Wilbur Evans as John, Fred Barry as Joe, Paul Reed as Peters and Daniel Nagrin as Daniel with dancers and singers; *Close as Pages in a Book* Wilbur Evans as John; *Opening* dancers; *The Fireman's Bride* Maureen Cannon as Rosie, Betty Bruce as Bessie, Fred Barry as Joe, Daniel Nagrin as Daniel with dancers and singers; *When the Party Gives a Party* singing girls and boys, Paul Reed as Peters, Rowan Tudor as Oakey Hall, James McElhoney as Monroe, Harry Meehan as Sweeney, Charles Irwin as Timothy and Walter Burke as Danny; *Maypole Dance* dancers; *Specialty* Fred Barry as Joe and Elaine Barry as Ellen; *The Big Back Yard* Wilbur Evans as John with singing girls and boys; *April Snow* Maureen Cannon as Rosie and Wilbur Evans as John; *Finaletto* dancers and singing girls and boys; *The Birds and the Bees* Maureen Cannon as Rosie, Charles Irwin as Timothy and Walter Burke as Danny; *Specialty* Betty Bruce as Bessie; *The Big Back Yard* orchestra; *Close as Pages in a Book* Mau-

---

[69] Starring Ted Ritter, *Stovepipe Hat* was produced in Los Angeles in 1961, with June Morris as the choreographer.

Up in Central Park, Broadway, cont
reen Cannon as Rosie and Wilbur Evans as John; *Finale* company

Staging of *Carrousel in the Park, Rip Van Winkle, The Fireman's Bride, The Big Back Yard* and *Finaletto,* Tamiris; staging of all other ensemble numbers, Lew Kesler; assistant to Tamiris, Daniel Nagrin

Singing Men: Phil Lowry, Charles W. Wood, Jerome Cardinale, Kenneth Renner, Leonard Daye, Stanley Turner, Bruce Lord, Bob Woodward, James Caputo, William Nuss, Rudy Rudisill, Harry Matlock, Sidney Paul and Michael Kozak

Men Dancers: Daniel Nagrin, Saul Bolasini, George Bockman, Henri Capri, Wally Coyle, Payne Converse and Robert Shaw

Singing Girls: Martha Burnett, Beatrice Lind, Mildred Jocelyn, Elyse Jahoda, Lillian Horn, Claire Saunders, Rose Marie Patane, Donna Hughes, Lydia Fredericks and Joan Gladding

Girl Dancers: Wana Allison, Joan Dubois, Margaret Gibson, Miriam Kornfield, Rebecca Lee, Ruth Lowe, Peggy Ann Nilsson, Hazel Roy, Evelyn Shaw, Gloria Stevens and Natalie Wynn

Up in Central Park

Touring history: Toured United States, 1946–47; toured Europe during World War II

Production details: production, Michael Todd; book, Herbert and Dorothy Fields; lyrics, Dorothy Fields; music, Sigmund Romberg; book staging, John Kennedy; dances, Helen Tamiris; settings and lighting, Howard Bay; costumes, Grace Houston and Ernest Schraps

Musical Program:[70] *Up from the Gutter* Betty Bruce as Bessie, Maureen Cannon as Rosie, Walter Burke as Danny, Russ Brown as Timothy with singers and dancers; *Carrousel in the Park* Maureen Cannon as Rosie; *It Doesn't Cost You Anything to Dream* Maureen Cannon as Rosie, Betty Bruce as Bessie and Earle MacVeigh as John; *Boss Tweed* Malcolm Lee Beggs as Tweed, Rowan Tudor as Oakey Hall, George Lane as Connolly, Harry Meehan as Sweeney, James Judson as Monroe, Stanley Noonan as Peters, Russ Brown as Timothy and men; *When She Walks in the Room* Earle MacVeigh as John; *Currier and Ives* Betty Bruce as Bessie and William H. Taft as Joe with George Bockman as George and dancers; *Close as Pages in a Book* Maureen Cannon as Bessie and Earle MacVeigh as John; *Rip Van Winkle* Maureen Cannon as Rosie, Betty Bruce as Bessie, Malcolm Lee Beggs as Tweed, Earle MacVeigh as John, William H. Taft as Joe, Stanley Noonan as Peters and George Bockman as George with singers and dancers; *Close as Pages in a Book* Earle MacVeigh as John; *Opening* dancers; *The Fireman's Bride* Maureen Cannon as Rosie, Betty Bruce as Bessie, William H. Taft as Joe, George Bockman as George with dancers and singers; *When the Party Gives a Party* singing girls and boys, Stanley Noonan as Peters, Rowan Tudor as Mayor Hall, James Judson as Monroe, Harry Meehan as Sweeney, Russ Brown as Timothy and Walter Burke as Danny; *Maypole Dance* dancers; *April Snow* Maureen Cannon as Rosie, Earle MacVeigh as John and singing girls and boys; *The Birds and the Bees* Maureen Cannon as Rosie, Betty Bruce as Bessie, Russ Brown as Timothy and Walter Burke as Danny; *Specialty* Betty Bruce as Bessie; *The Big Back Yard* orchestra and ensemble; *Close as Pages in a Book* Maureen Cannon as Rosie and Earle MacVeigh as John; *Finale* company. Staging of *Carrousel in the Park, Rip Van Winkle, The Fireman's Bride,* and *The Big Back Yard,* Tamiris; staging of all other ensemble numbers, Lew Kesler

Dancing girls: Marjory Bradford, Isabelle Chase, Virginia Conwell, Anna Friedland, Spicy Gillen, Joan Grosse, Ruth Lowe, June Maclaren, Gloria Michaels, Joanne Stone and Patsy Wymore

Dancing boys: George Bockman (captain), Ray Arnett, Robert Billheimer, Wally Coyle, Kenneth Owen, Dick Trevorrah and Louis Yetter

Singing girls: Mary Allen, Eloise Anderson, Betty Halperin, Eve Harvey, Shirley Neu-

---

[70] This touring history information is taken from Nov 8–9 1946 program in St Paul Auditorium, St Paul, Minnesota.

mann, Janet Roland, Ann Shier, Mary Jane Woerver and Lillian Withington.

Singing boys: John Allocca, Oren Dabbs, Paul Durham, Leonard Ellison, Joseph Fazio, Seymour Heller, Dick Hughes, Edward Pate, Hobart Streiford, Joseph Zaro, Bernard Zwarg and John Thorne

Others: Guy Standing Jr as Thomas Nast, John Quigg as William Dutton, Gloria Folland as Lotta Stevens, Lilias MacLellan as Clara Manning, Jack Howard as James Fiske Jr, Louise Holden as Maid and Governess and Joanne and Janet Lally as children

Up in Central Park

Motion picture, Universal International, 1948

Production details: production and screenplay, Karl Tunberg; direction, William Seiter; photographer, Milton Krasner; musical direction, Johnny Green; dances, Helen Tamiris; costumes, Mary Grant

Cast: Deanna Durbin as Rosie Moore, Dick Haymes as John Matthews, Vincent Price as Boss Tweed, Albert Sharpe as Timothy Moore, Tom Powers as Rogan, Hobart Cavanaugh as Mayor Oakley, Thurston Hall as Gov. Motley, Howard Freeman as Schultz and the Helen Tamiris Dancers including William Skipper, Nelle Fisher and others

New Production of Show Boat

Broadway history: Opened Jan 5 1946   New York: Ziegfield Theatre
Closed Jan 4 1947 after 418 performances

Production details: production, Jerome Kern and Oscar Hammerstein 2nd; book and lyrics, Oscar Hammerstein 2nd; music, Jerome Kern; staging, Hassard Short; novel, Edna Ferber; dances, Helen Tamiris; settings, Howard Bay; costumes, Lucinda Ballard

Musical Program: *Cotton Blossom*, company; *Show Boat Parade* and *Ballyhoo* Ralph Dumke as Capt. Andy with the show boat troupe and townspeople; *Only Make Believe* Charles Fredericks as Ravenal and Jan Clayton as Magnolia; *Ol' Man River* Kenneth Spencer as Joe with stevedores; *Can't Help Lovin' Dat Man* Carol Bruce as Julie, Helen Dowdy as Queenie, Jan Clayton as Magnolia, Kenneth Spencer as Joe with quartette; *Life Upon the Wicked Stage* Collette Lyons as Ellie and stage door admirers with dance *No Gems, No Rose, No Gentlemen; Ballyhoo* Helen Dowdy as Queenie and ensemble with dance *No Shoes* Pearl Primus as Sal, Laverne French as Sam and theatre goers; *You Are Love* Jan Clayton as Magnolia and Charles Fredericks as Ravenal; *Finale* company with *Levee Dance* Talley Beatty as Talley, Claude Marchant as Claude and Laverne French as Sam and levee dancers; *At the Fair* sightseers, barkers and ushers with dance *Congress of Beauties* ushers and beauties Andrea Downing as Spanish, Vivian Cherry as Italian, Janice Bodenhoff as French, Elana Keller as Scotch, Audrey Keane as Greek, Marta Becket as English, Olga Lunick as Russian and Eleanor Boleyn as Indian; *Why Do I Love You?* Jan Clayton as Magnolia, Charles Fredericks as Ravenal and ensemble; *In Dahomey* Dahomey village with dances *Dance of the Dahomeys* and *Avenue A Release* Pearl Primus as Dahomey Queen, villagers and the bewitched Alma Sutton as Ata, Claude Marchant as Mala and Talley Beatty as Bora; *Bill* Carol Bruce as Julie; *Can't Help Lovin' Dat Man* Jan Clayton as Magnolia; *Service and Scene Music, St Agatha's Convent; Only Make Believe* Charles Fredericks as Ravenal; "*Goodbye, My Love*" *Cake Walk* Buddy Ebson as Frank and Colette Lyons as Ellie; Magnolia's Debut in Tracadero Music Hall: "*After the Ball*" Jan Clayton as Magnolia; *Ol' Man River* Kenneth Spencer as Joe; *You are Love* Charles Fredericks as Ravenal; *Nobody Else But Me* Alyce Mace as Kim with *Dance 1927* Alyce Mace as Kim, Charles Tate as Jimmy and flappers, cake eaters and levee dancers; *Finale* company

Assistant to Tamiris, Daniel Nagrin; choral director, Pembroke Davenport

Girl singers: Carmine Alexandria, Grace Brenton, Clarise Crawford, Lydia Fredericks, Adah Friley, Marion Hairston, Katie Hall,

Show Boat, Broadway, cont
  Marion Holaves, Jean Jones, Frances Joslyn, Charlotte Junius, Assota Marshall, Linda Mason, Eulabel Riley, Agnes Sundgren, Bettina Thayer, Fannie Turner, Ethel Brown White and Evelyn Wick

Boy singers: Jerome Addison, Gilbert Adkins, Ivory Bass, William Bender, Tom Bowman, Robert Bulger, Edward Chappel, William Cole, Erno Czako, Richard Di Silvera, John Garth III, Hayes Gordon, George H. Hall, Robert Kimberly, James Lapsley, Albert McCary, William McDaniel, Bowling H. Mansfield, Walter Mosby, Clarence Redd, Paul Shiers, William C. Smith, William Sol, Rodester Timmons and David Trimble

Girl dancers: Marta Becket, Elmira Jones Bey, Janice Bodenhoff, Eleanor Boleyn, Vivian Cherry, Andrea Downing, Betty Jane Geiskopf, Carol Harriton, Vickie Henderson, Audrey Keane, Elana Keller, Ora Leak, Olga Lunick, Jeanne Reeves, Alma Sutton, Viola Taylor and Yvonne Tibor

Boy dancers: Talley Beatty, Terry Dawson, LaVerne French, Eddie Howland, Gerard Leavitt, Claude Marchant, William Miller, Nick Nadeau, Joe Nash, Stanley Simmons, William Weber, Henry Wessel and Francisco Xavier.

Captain: Paula Kaye

Children: Betty Barker, Dolores Gamble, Carol Lewis, Miriam Quinn, Sybil Stocking, Billy De Forest, Roland Gamble, Edward Hayes, Bobby O'Connor and Eugene Steiner

City Center Production of Show Boat

Opened Sept 7 1948 after 16 performances   New York: City Center   Closed Sept 18 1948

Production details: production, Jerome Kern and Oscar Hammerstein 2nd; book and lyrics, Oscar Hammerstein 2nd; music, Jerome Kern; staging, Hassard Short; novel, Edna Ferber; dances, Helen Tamiris; settings, Howard Bay; costumes, Lucinda Ballard

Musical Program: *Cotton Blossom,* company; *Show Boat Parade* and *Ballyhoo* Billy House as Capt Andy with the show boat troupe and townspeople; *Only Make Believe* Norwood Smith as Ravenal and Pamela Caveness as Magnolia; *Ol' Man River* Wm C. Smith as Joe with stevedores; *Can't Help Lovin' Dat Man* Carol Bruce as Julie, Helen Dowdy as Queenie, Pamela Caveness as Magnolia, Wm C. Smith as Joe with quartette; *Life Upon the Wicked Stage* Clare Alden as Ellie and stage door admirers with dance *No Gems, No Roses, No Gentlemen; Ballyhoo* Helen Dowdy as Queenie and ensemble with dance *No Shoes* Gloria Smith as Sal, Laverne French as Sam and theatre goers; *You Are Love* Pamela Caveness as Magnolia and Norwood Smith as Ravenal; *Finale* company with *Levee Dance* Reggie, Jimmie, George and Levee Dancers; *At the Fair* sightseers, barkers, ushers with dance *Congress of Beauties* ushers and beauties; *Why Do I Love You?* Pamela Caveness as Magnolia, Norwood Smith as Ravenal and ensemble; *In Dahomey* Dahomey village with dances *Dance of the Dahomeys* and *Avenue A Release* Laverne French as Dahomey King and Dahomey Dancers; *Bill* Terry Saunders as Julie; *Can't Help Lovin' Dat Man* Pamela Caveness as Magnolia; *Service and Scene Music,* St Agatha's Convent; *Only Make Believe* Norwood Smith as Ravenal; *"Goodbye, My Love" Cake Walk* Sammy White as Frank and Clare Alden as Ellie; Magnolia's Debut in Tracadero Music Hall: *"After the Ball"* Pamela Caveness as Magnolia; *Ol' Man River* Wm C. Smith as Joe; *You Are Love* Norwood Smith as Ravenal; *Nobody Else But Me* Alyce Mace as Kim with *Dance 1927* Alyce Mace as Kim, Sheldon Bennett as Jimmy and flappers, cake eaters and levee dancers; *Finale* company

Information on singers and dancers unavailable

Annie Get Your Gun

Broadway history: Opened May 16 1946   New York: Imperial Theatre   Closed Feb 12 1949 after 1,147 performances   Opened Feb

Miss Tamiris on Broadway, 1944-1955

19 1958   New York: City Center performances   Closed Mar 2 1958 after 15

Production details: production, Richard Rodgers and Oscar Hammerstein 2nd; book, Herbert and Dorothy Fields; music and lyrics, Irving Berlin; dances, Helen Tamiris; sets and lighting, Jo Mielziner; costumes, Lucinda Ballard; direction, Joshua Logan

Musical Program: *Buffalo Bill* Marty May as Charlie and ensemble; *I'm a Bad, Bad Man* Ray Middleton as Frank with girls, danced by Duncan Noble, Paddy Stone, Parker Wilson and ensemble; *Doin' What Comes Naturally* Ethel Merman as Annie, Art Barnett as Foster Wilson and Annie's sisters and brother; *The Girl That I Marry* Ray Middleton as Frank; *You Can't Get a Man With a Gun* Ethel Merman as Annie; *Show Business* William O'Neal as Buffalo Bill, Marty May as Charlie, Ray Middleton as Frank and Ethel Merman as Annie; *They Say It's Wonderful* Ray Middleton as Frank and Ethel Merman as Annie; *Moonshine Lullaby* Ethel Merman as Annie and trio; *I'll Share It All with You* Betty Anne Nyman as Winnie and Kenny Bowers as Tommy; *"Ballyhoo"* Lubov Roudenko as Riding Mistress and show people; *Show Business* Ethel Merman as Annie; *My Defenses Are Down* Ray Middleton as Frank and boys; *Wild Horse Ceremonial Dance* Daniel Nagrin as The Wild Horse with braves and maidens; *I'm an Indian Too* Ethel Merman as Annie; *Adoption Dance* Ethel Merman as Annie, Daniel Nagrin as The Wild Horse and braves; *Lost in His Arms* Ethel Merman as Annie and ensemble; *Who Do You Love, I Hope?* Betty Anne Nyman as Winnie and Kenny Bowers as Tommy, danced by Betty Anne Nyman, Kenny Bowers and ensemble; *Sun in the Morning* Ethel Merman as Annie and ensemble, danced by Lubov Roudenko, Daniel Nagrin and show people; *They Say It's Wonderful* Ethel Merman as Annie and Ray Middleton as Frank; *The Girl That I Marry* Ray Middleton as Frank; *Anything You Can Do* Ethel Merman as Annie and Ray Middleton as Frank; *Show Business* company

Assistant to Tamiris, Daniel Nagrin

Singing girls: Truly Barbara, Ellen Hanley, Ostrid Lind, Jet MacDonald, Dorothy Richards, Ruth Strickland, Katrina Van Oss, Marietta Vore, Ruth Vrana and Mary Woodley

Singing boys: Jack Byron, Robert Dixon, Bernard Griffin, Marvin Goodis, Noel Gordon, Vincent Henry, Don Liberto, Fred Rivett, Earl Vauvain and Rob Taylor

Dancing girls: Franca Baldwin, Tessie Carrano, Madeleine Detry, Cyprienne Gabelman, Barbara Gaye, Evelyn Giles, Mary Grey and Harriet Roeder

Dancing boys: Jack Beaber, John Begg, Michael Maule, Duncan Noble, Jack Pierce, Paddy Stone, Ken Whelan and Parker Wilson

London Production of Annie Get Your Gun

Opened June 7 1947   London: Coliseum

Production details: production, Helen Tamiris and Charles Hickman; direction and choreography, Helen Tamiris; assistant to Tamiris, Daniel Nagrin

Cast: Dolores Gray as Annie, Bill Johnson as Frank, Hal Bryan as Charlie Davenport, John Garside as Chief Sitting Bull, Paddy Stone as Iron Tail and Wild Horse Ceremonial Dancer, Ellis Irving as Col Wm. F. Cody, Patricia Garnett as Riding Mistress, John Crossfield as Timothy Gardner, Noel Hurst as Clyde Smith and Mr Lockwood, Keith Lee as John, John Milburn as Freddie and Dr John Ferguson, John R. Singer as Pawnee's Messenger, James Clark as Major Domo, Bernard Quinn as Mr Schuyler Adams, Marguerite Earle as Mrs Schuyler Adams, Mark Pasquin as Mr Ernest Henderson, Elizabeth St Denis as Mrs Ernest Henderson, Betty Hare as Sylvia Potter-Porter; Joan Grundy as Girl in Pink; Sidney Kellham as Yellow Foot, William Thompson as Mac, Hal Osmond as Foster Wilson and Mr Clay, Jack Griffin as Coolie, Barbara Babington as Dolly Tate, Wendy Toye as Winnie Tate, Irving Davies as Tommy Keeler, Dorothy Black as Girl with Bouquet and Nancy, Perlita Neilson as Minnie, Marian Chapman as Jessie, Faith Bailey as Nellie, Michael Nichols as Little Jake, David Griffith as Harry and Andy Turner, Brenda

Annie Get Your Gun, London, cont
Gayle as Mrs Percy Ferguson, Doris Fishwick as Mrs Little Horse, Marietta Buttery as Mrs Black Tooth, Jose Marnia as Mrs Yellow Foot, James Clark as Trainman, Vic Brown as Waiter, Don Johnson as Porter, Edmund Dalby as Major Gordon Lillie, Elaine Giles as Mabel, Hetty Ward as Louise and Dennis Peck as Little Boy, Sally Mayo as Little Girl

Annie Get Your Gun

Touring History: Opened Oct 3 1947
Toured 1947–48 in United States

Dallas: Fair Park Auditorium

Production details: dances by Helen Tamiris; recreation of dances, Daniel Nagrin

Cast: Mary Martin as Annie, Earl Covert as Frank, Barton Mumaw as The Wild Horse, Tessie Corrano as The Riding Mistress, Billie Worth as Winnie, Tommy Wonder as Tommy, Donald Burr as Charlie, Jack Rutherford as Buffalo Bill, Forrest Carter as Freddie and Edwin Clay as Foster Wilson

Featured dancers: Regis Powers, John Hurdle and Merritt Thompson

Singing girls and boys: Frances Darrell, Barbara Davis, Mary Della Rosa, Helena Dudas, Jane Judge, Gloria Meli, Christine Bagaloff, Sandra Deel, Carolyn Hunter and Zosia Gruchala; William Goonan, Forrest Carter, Paul Grady, Vincent Lubrano, Oren Dabbs, John Dorrin, Harry Brose, Darrell Perkins, Robert Caldwell and Hobart Streitford

Dancing girls and boys: Rita Charise, Gloria Charles, Beverly Bithell, Ann Deasy, Charlotte Leslie, Dolores Samonsky, Ingrid Secretan and Doris Wright; Paul D'Amboise, John Hurdle, Kenneth Laurence, William Miller, Regis Powers, Abel Pokras, Joey Thomas, Merritt Thompson and Robert Thompson

City Center Production of Annie Get Your Gun

Opened Feb 19 1958 after 15 performances

New York: City Center

Closed Mar 2 1958

Dances and staging of musical numbers, Helen Tamiris

Cast: Betty Jane Watson as Annie, David Atkinson as Frank, Stuart Hodes as Iron Horse and The Wild Horse, Ruthanna Boris as Riding Mistress, Rain Winslow as Winnie, Richard France as Tommie, Jack Whiting as Charlie, James Rennie as Buffalo Bill and Leo Lucker as Foster Wilson

Dancers: Joan Dubrow, Beverly Gains, Lida Gaschke, Dorothy Hill, Iva March, Miriam Pandor, Fleur Raup, Rene Slade, Carolee Winchester, Doris Wright, Allan Byrns, Marvin Gordon, Charles Jackson, Daniel Jogalsky, Edward Monson, James Moore, Harold Pittard, Parker Wilson and Vic Vallaro[71]

Park Avenue

Broadway history: Opened Nov 4 1946
Closed Jan 4 1947 after 72 performances

New York: Shubert Theatre

Production details: production, Max Gordon; book, Nunnally Johnson and George S. Kaufman; lyrics, Ira Gershwin; music, Arthur Schwartz; dances and musical numbers, Helen Tamiris; settings and lighting, Donald Oenslager; gowns (except leading lady), Tina Leser

Musical Program: *Tomorrow Is the Time* bridesmaids; *For the Life of Me* Ray McDonald as Ned and Martha Stewart as Madge, danced by Ray McDonald as Ned, Martha Stewart as Madge, William Skipper as James, Harold Mattox as Ted and bridesmaids; *The Dew Was on the Rose* Leonora

---

[71] With dances almost banished from the story, Metro-Goldwyn-Mayer did put out a motion picture of *Annie Get Your Gun* in 1950, choreography by Robert Alton (Betty Hutton played Annie and Howard Keel played Frank Butler).

Corbett as Sybil, Arthur Margetson as Oggie, Charles Purcell as Reggie, Raymond Walburn as Richard and Robert Chisholm as Charles; *Don't Be a Woman If You Can* Dorothy Bird as Betty, Marthe Errolle as Elsa and Ruth Matteson as Myra; *Sweet Nevada* Leonora Corbett as Sybil and David Wayne as Mr Meachem with dance *"In the Courtroom"* Dorothy Bird as Laura, Joan Mann as Beverly, Betty Low as Brenda, David Wayne as Mr Meachem, William Skipper as James, Harold Mattox as Ted and "All Brendas" Adelle Rasey, Sherry Shadburne, Carol Chandler, Betty Ann Lynn, Kyle MacDonald, Eileen Coffman, June Graham, Betty Low, Virginia Morris, Judi Blacque, Gloria Anderson and Margaret Gibson; *There's No Holding Me* Martha Stewart as Madge and Ray McDonald as Ned; *The Dew Was on the Rose* Leonora Corbett as Sybil and Arthur Margetson as Oggie; *There's Nothing Like Marriage for People* company; *Hope for the Best* Martha Stewart as Madge, Marthe Errole as Elsa, Mary Wickes as Betty, and Ruth Matteson as Myra; *My Son-in-Law* Leonora Corbett as Sybil, Raymond Walburn as Richard, Charles Purcell as Reggie and Robert Chisholm as Charles; *Land of Opportunities* Arthur Margetson as Oggie, Raymond Walburn as Richard, Charles Purcell as Reggie and Robert Chisholm as Charles, danced by Dorothy Bird as Laura, Joan Mann as Beverly and "All Brendas" Sherry Shadburne, Carol Chandler, Betty Ann Lynn, Kyle MacDonald, Eileen Coffman, June Graham, Betty Low, Virginia Morris, Judi Blacque, Gloria Anderson and Margaret Gibson; *Goodbye to All That* Martha Stewart as Madge and Ray McDonald as Ned with dance *Echo* Harold Mattox as Ted, Dorothy Bird as Laura, William Skipper as James, Joan Mann as Beverly and bridesmaids; *Finale*, company

Assistants to Tamiris, Dorothy Bird and Daniel Nagrin; musical adaptation for dances, Clay Warnick

The Great Campaign

Broadway history: Opened March 30 1947 for five performances New York: Princess Theatre

Production details: sponsorship, American National Theatre and Academy, The Experimental Theatre, Inc; production, T. Edward Hambleton; book, Arnold Sundgaard; staging, Joseph Losey; associate direction, Helen Tamiris; music, Alex North; settings, Robert Davison; choreography, Anna Sokolow; costumes, Rose Bogdanoff

Cast: Kay Loring as Emily Trellis, Millard Mitchell as Sam Trellis, Thomas Coley as Jeff Trellis, John Eaton as Trivett, Clara Cordery as Jane, Ruth Rowen as Paula, Philip Robinson as Wilderness, Howard Brockway as Trumpeter, John O'Shaughnessy as Mr Cook, Ray Boyle as Kenneth, Mary Lou Taylor as Kenneth's Girl, Frances Waller as Laneth, Glen Tetley as Barber, Alan Manson as Henry, William Roerick as John, Robert P. Lieb as Wallie P. Hale, Erik Rhodes as Sidney Gat, Robert Alvin as Roscoe Dray, Paul Bain as Hamp, Marsh McLeod as Laura, Gayne Sullivan as Eddie, Ann d'Autremont as Anna, Howard Wendell as Avery

Dancers: Clara Cordery, Margaret McCallion, Ruth Rowen, Solvei Wiberg, Richard Astor, John Eaton and Glen Tetley

Scenes: Minnesota; Illinois; Columbus; Zanesville; Columbus; U.S.A.; Zanesville; Illinois; U.S.A.; Minnesota; Columbus; Illinois; Columbus; Minnesota

The Promised Valley[72]

Production history: Opened July 21 1947   Salt Lake City, Utah: Stadium Bowl   Closed Aug 9 1947 after 18 performances

Production details: production, Utah Centennial Commission: books and lyrics, Arnold Sundgaard; music, Crawford Gates; dances, Helen Tamiris; musical direction, Jay Black-

---

[72] This material is taken from the souvenir program in the Utah State Archives, State Capitol, Salt Lake City, Utah.

The Promised Valley, cont
ton; direction, C. Lowell Lees; costumes, Sereta T. Jones

Musical numbers: *Prologue* Richard Davies as Leader, Mormon Scouts, Boys' Choir and chorus with dance sequences by Virginia Tanner, Joseph Gifford, Sue Remos and ensemble; *The Shirt Song* Ross B. Ramsey as Fennelly Parsons with his sons played by Joseph Bywater, Alden Richards, David Morgan, Royal Nielson, Robert Critchlow, Stephen Olsen, William McConahay and Michael Thomas; *The Wind Is a Lion* Jet MacDonald as Celia Faraday Cutler; *Love Is My Song* Jet MacDonald as Celia and chorus; *I Dream of a Valley Home* Jet MacDonald as Celia and Alfred Drake as Jedediah Cutler; *The Upper California* chorus with dance sequences by Virginia Tanner, Joseph Gifford, Sue Remos, Maia Yarrick and ensemble; *Sparking on a Sunday Night* sung by Gae Peterson and Neil W. Neilson and danced by Nelle Fisher and Barton Mumaw; *The Wind Is a Lion* Jet MacDonald as Celia and Alfred Drake as Jed and chorus; *Come, Come Ye Saints* chorus; *The Wind Is a Lion* Alfred Drake as Jed and Jet MacDonald as Celia and chorus; *My Heart Is Lost and Lonely* Alfred Drake as Jed and Jet MacDonald as Celia; *Come, Come Ye Saints* chorus; *The Cushioned Seat* Ross B. Ramsey as Fennelly; *This Is the Place* The sons played by Alden Richards, Joseph Bywater, David Morgan, Royal Nielson, Robert Critchlow, Stephen Olsen, William McConahay, Michael Thomas with Richard Davies as Leader and Boys' Choir; *The Choir Practice Song* Jet MacDonald as Celia and chorus; *My Heart Is Lost and Lonely* Jet MacDonald as Celia; *It's So Good to Be Home Again* Alfred Drake as Jed with Mormon Battalion; *Love Is My Song* Jet MacDonald as Celia and Alfred Drake as Jed with chorus; *Think Not When You Gather to Zion* Ross B. Ramsey as Fennelly; *Golly, I'm Glad to Be Alive* Ross B. Ramsey as Fennelly with sons played by Alden Richards, Joseph Bywater, David Morgan, Royal Nielson, Robert Critchlow, Stephen Olsen, William McConahay and Michael Thomas; *I Wonder Why* Alfred Drake as Jed; *Indian Chant* with drum solo by Joseph Mallory; *The Wind Is a Lion* Jet MacDonald as Celia; *Cricket-Gull Choral-Ballet* Alfred Drake as Jed, Richard Davies as Leader and chorus; *Epilogue* Richard Davies as Leader, Alfred Drake as Jed, Jet MacDonald as Celia, Ross B. Ramsey as Fennelly, Boys' Choir and chorus

Additional cast: Lila Eccles Brimhall as Emma Faraday, Ross Dalton as Caleb Faraday, Gordon Low and Louis Mallory as Milom and Lorenzo, Robert Hyde Wilson as Jamie Logan, Stanley Russon as Brother Zarabel, Wayne Richards as Brother Willis and Brother Rawson, John Nicolaysen as Colonel John Broderick, Nelle Fisher as Indian Princess, Barton Mumaw as Young Chief and Ruth Weller as Mrs Parsons

Solo Dancers: Joseph Gifford, Sue Remos, Virginia Tanner and Maia Yarrick. Dancers: Beverly Bithell, Maxcine Glaudin, Alice Cannon, Betty Durham, Elaine Erickson, Charles Hamm, Henry Kirsh, Helene Lund, Marjorie Merrill, Caroll Moffat, Barshaw Murphy, Nonie Nelson, Marlene Peacock, Bill Pillich, Gloria Rosoff, Paul Suchman, Louella Swensen and Juan Valenzuela

Inside U. S. A.

Broadway history: Opened Apr 30 1948   New York: New Century Theatre   Closed Feb 19 1949 after 339 performances

Production details: production, Arthur Schwartz; original book, John Gunther; sketches, Arnold Auerbach, Moss Hart and Arnold B. Horwitt; lyrics and music, Howard Dietz and Arthur Schwartz; incidental music for dances, Genevieve Pitot; production associate, Victor Samrock; dances and staging of musical numbers, Helen Tamiris; production designer, Lemuel Ayers; sketches director, Robert H. Gordon; costumes, Eleanor Goldsmith and Castillo

Revue Numbers: *Inside U. S. A.* company; *Leave My Pulse Alone* (Any Town, Coast-to-Coast) Estelle Loring as Lottie the maid, Carl Reiner as 1st Pollster, Jane Lawrence as Mrs Jones, Jack Haley as Mr Jones, Lewis Nye as 2nd Pollster, Beverlee Bozeman as Mary the daughter and William LeMassena as 3rd Pollster; *Come, O Come* (Pittsburgh) Beatrice Lillie as Choral Director of Pittsburgh Choral Society; *Forty Winks* (Miami Beach) Jack Haley as Mr Bemis, William LeMassena as Hotel Manager, Lewis Nye as Bellboy and Carl Reiner as Prof Poultergeist; *Blue Grass* (Churchill Downs, Kentucky) sung by Thelma Carpenter and danced by Albert Popwell Her Boy Friend and J. C. McCord as His Friend with Rod Alexander, Rally Beatty, Beverlee Bozeman, Michael Charnley, Ronald Chetwood, Jacqueline Fisher, Bob Hamilton, Holly Harris, Pat Horn, Norma Larkin, Mara Lynn, Dorothy MacNeill, Joan Mann, Manon Millis, John Mooney, Betty Nichols, Richard Reed, George Reich, Ricky Riccardi, Thomas Reider, Boris Rumanin, Dorothy Scott, Sherry Shadburne, Gloria Stevens and Royce Wallace as Bookies, Spectators and Jockeys; *A Song to Forget* (Chillicothe, Ohio) Beatrice Lillie as Miss Twitchell, Carl Reiner as Frederic Chopin, William LeMassena as a Butler, Beatrice Lillie as Mme Lapis de Lazuli, John Tyers as Franz Liszt and Lewis Nye as Peter Illyitch Tschaikowsky; *Rhode Island Is Famous for You* sung by Jack Haley and Estelle Loring; *Haunted Heart* (San Francisco) sung by John Tyers and danced by Valerie Bettis with J. C. McCord, George Reich and Rod Alexander; *Massachusetts Mermaid* Beatrice Lillie; *A Feller from Indiana* Herb Shriner; *First Prize at the Fair* (Wisconsin) William LeMassena as Ticket Seller, Jane Lawrence and Ray Stephens as 1st Couple, Estelle Loring and Jim Hawthorne as 2nd Couple, Beatrice Lillie and Jack Haley as 3rd Couple and Eric Victor as Caller and rest of company as Contestants and Spectators; *At the Mardi Gras* (New Orleans) sung by Beatrice Lillie with Jack Cassidy, Jim Hawthorne, Alfred Homan, Thomas Rieder, Michael Risk and Raymond Stephens as Six Swains and danced by Rod Alexander, Tally Beatty, Ricky Riccardi, Beverlee Bozeman, Michael Charnley, Ronald Chetwood, Robert Hamilton, Pat Horn, Mara Lynn, Joan Mann, J. C. McCord, Manon Millis, Betty Nichols, Albert Popwell, Richard Reed, George Reich, Boris Runanin, Dorothy Scott, Gloria Stevens and Royce Wallace; *School for Waiters* (New York City) Joan Mann as Girl, Carl Reiner as Man, Jack Haley as Professor, Lewis Nye as Herman, Jane Lawrence as Girl Diner, William LeMassena as Her Escort, Carl Reiner as Another Diner, Holly Harris and Hilde Palmer as His Companions, Ronald Chetwood as Captain of Waiters and Rod Alexander, Court Fleming, Richard Reed, George Reich and Boris Runanin as Student Waiters; *My Gal Is Mine Once More* (Wyoming) sung by John Tyers as Groom, Estelle Loring as Bride, Carl Reiner as Minister, J. C. McCord as Cowboy with Rope and Mary Lou Boyd, Beverlee Bozeman, Jack Cassidy, Jim Hawthorne, Norma Larkin, Mara Lynn, Dorothy MacNeil, Joan Mann, J. C. McCord, John Mooney, Thomas Rieder, Michael Risk, Dorothy Scott, Sherry Shadburne, Raymond Stephens and Gloria Stevens as Townspeople; *Better Luck Next Time* (Just Off Broadway) Jane Lawrence as Mary Shelton, Beatrice Lillie as Gladys her maid and Randell Henderson as The Stage Manager; *Tiger Lily* (Chicago) (A tabloid ballet conceived by Helen Tamiris) Valerie Bettis as Tiger Lily, Eric Victor as Doctor Zilmore, Rod Alexander, Robert Hamilton, J. C. McCord and Richard Reed as Detectives, Rod Alexander as Prosecuting Attorney, Ronald Chetwood as Defense Attorney, Tally Beatty, Gloria Stevens, Robert Hamilton, Joan Mann, J. C. McCord and Boris Runanin as Jury, Carl Reiner as Judge and Beverlee Bozeman, Jack Cassidy, Jacqueline Fisher, Court Fleming, Holly Harris, Jim Hawthorne, Alfred Homan, Pat Horn, Norma Larkin, William LeMassena, Mara Lynn, Nanon Millis, John Mooney, Betty Nichols, George Reich, Richard Reed, Ricky Riccardi, Thomas Rieder, Michael Risk, Dorothy Scott, Sherry Shadburne, Raymond Stephens, Gloria Stevens and Royce Wallace as Newspaper Readers and Spectators; *We Won't Take It Back* (Albuquerque, New Mexico) sung by Beatrice Lillie and Jack Haley with Alfred Homan, Jane Lawrence, William LeMassena, Carl Reiner, Lewis Nye and Hilde Palmer as Tourists; *Finale* company

Assistant to Tamiris, Daniel Nagrin

Touch and Go

Broadway history: Opened Oct 13 1949   New York: Broadhurst Theatre   Closed Mar 18 1950 after 176 performances

Production details: production, George Abbott; sketches and lyrics, Jean and Walter Kerr; music, Jay Gorney; ballet music, Genevieve Pitot; direction, Walter Kerr; chore-

Touch and Go, cont

ography, Helen Tamiris; production design, John Robert Lloyd; lighting, Peggy Clark; musical direction, Antonio Morelli

Revue Numbers: *An Opening for Everybody* George Hall, Helen Gallagher, Jonathan Lucas and the company as Theatregoers; *This Had Better Be Love* Nancy Andrews and Dick Sykes; *Gorilla Girl* George Hall as Director, Art Carroll as Assistant Director, Kyle MacDonnell as Miss Hilton, Jonathan Lucas as Skeets, Lewis Nye as Trainer and Nat Frey as Cameraman; *American Primitive* (Funny Little Old World) sung by Muriel O'Malley with Art Carroll as Father and Helen Gallagher as Daughter and danced by Pearl Lang and Daniel Nagrin and Greb Lober, David Lober, Richard Reed, William Sumner, Beverly Tassoni, Merritt Thompson, Dorothy Scott and Parker Wilson; *Highbrow, Lowbrow* Dick Sykes, Jonathan Lucas and Larry Robbins; *Disenchantment* George Hall as Muffins, Dick Sykes as Old Gent (pippy), Peggy Cass as Moonbeam, William Sumner as Newsboy, Lewis Nye as Papa and Larry Robbins as Pilgrim; *Easy Does It* Helen Gallagher as The Girl, Daniel Nagrin as The Man, David Lober as The Other Man, Eleanor Boleyn and Greb Lober as The Girl Friends and the company; *Be a Mess* Peggy Cass as Olivia, Nancy Andrews as Barbara and Kyle MacDonnell as Jane; *Broadway Love Song* danced by Pearl Lang and Jonathan Lucas; *It'll Be All Right in a Hundred Years* Art Carroll as Boy and Kyle MacDonnell as Girl; *Great Dane A-Comin'* Ray Page as King, Nancy Andrews as Queen, Dick Sykes as Hamlet, Daniel Nagrin as Laertes, Kyle MacDonnell as Ophelia, George Hall as Polonius and company; *Wish Me Luck* sung by Nancy Andrews with David Lober as Croupier and danced by the company; *What It Was Really Like* Nat Frey as 1st Aide, Lewis Nye as 2nd Aide, Dick Sykes as General, Larry Robbins as Malloy, George Hall as C O and Jonathan Lucas as Kerrigan; *Under the Sleeping Volcano* sung by Pearl Hacker, Lydia Fredericks, Arlyne Frank and Beverly Purvin and danced by Ilona Murrai as Carita's Sister, Pearl Lang as Carita, Daniel Nagrin as Felipe, David Lober as Francesco and Dorothy Scott, Eleanor Boleyn, Beverly Tassoni, Greb Lober, William Sumner, Parker Wilson, Merritt Thompson, Richard Reed and George Reich as Villagers; *Men of the Water-Mark* Art Carroll, Nat Frey, George Hall, Carl Nicholas, Louis Nye and Larry Robbins; *Mr Brown, Miss Dupree* Kyle MacDonnell as Miss Dupree, Muriel O'Malley as Mama and Jonathan Lucas as Mr Brown and danced by Mary Anthony, Ilona Murrai, Beverly Tassoni, Dorothy Scott, David Lober, Richard Reed, George Reich and Merritt Thompson; *Miss Platt Selects Mate* Nancy Andrews; *Cinderella* Muriel O'Malley as Stepmother, Helen Gallagher as Neighbor, Nancy Andrews as 1st Sister, Peggy Cass as 2nd Sister, Kyle MacDonnell as Cinderella, Jonathan Lucas as Newsboy, Lewis Nye as Prince and Larry Robbins as Page; *Finale* company

Assistant to Tamiris, Daniel Nagrin

Others in cast: Bobby Trelease and Mara Lynn

Great to Be Alive

Broadway history: Opened Mar 23 1950 Closed May 6 1950 after 52 performances New York: Winter Garden

Production details: production, Vinton Freedley in association with Anderson Lawler and Russell Markert; book, Walter Bullock and Sylvia Regan; lyrics, Walter Bullock; music, Abraham Ellstein; direction, Mary Hunter; dances and staging of musical numbers, Helen Tamiris; settings, costumes and lighting, Stewart Chaney; musical direction, Max Meth

Musical Program: *When the Sheets Come Back from the Laundry* Valerie Bettis as Kitty, Bambi Linn as Bonnie, Betty Low as Prudence, Aleen Buchanan as Maybelle, Rod Alexander as Albert, J. C. McCord as Jake, Jay Marshall as Crumleigh and dancers Eleanor Fairchild, Eleanore Gregory, Barbara Heath, Ann Hutchinson, Norma Kaiser, Janice Rule, Chuck Brunner, Ted Cappy, Roscoe French, David Nillo, Harry Rogers and Swen Swenson; *It's a Long Time Till Tomorrow* Martha Wright as Carol and Mark Dawson as Vince; *Headin' for a Weddin'* Stuart Erwin as Twigg, Valerie Bettis as Kitty, Bambi Linn as Bonnie, Betty Low as Prudence, Aleen Buchanan as Maybelle, Rod Alexander as Albert, J. C.

McCord as Jake, Jay Marshall as Crumleigh and dancers Eleanor Fairchild, Eleanore Gregory, Barbara Heath, Ann Hutchinson, Norma Kaiser, Janice Rule, Chuck Brunner, Ted Cappy, Roscoe French, David Nillo, Harry Rogers and Swen Swenson; *Redecorate* Earl Oxford as Butch; *What a Day!* Martha Wright as Carol, Mark Dawson as Vince, Virginia Curtis as Blodgett, Jeanne Bal as Sandra, Russell Nype as Freddie and Guests; *Call It Love* Martha Wright as Carol and Mark Dawson as Vince; *There's Nothing Like It* Virginia Curtis as Blodgett; *Dreams Ago* Martha Wright as Carol and Mark Dawson as Vince with dances *Waltz* Bambi Linn as Bonnie and Rod Alexander as Albert and *The Story of Kitty* Valerie Bettis as Kitty, David Nillo as Jonathan and dancers Eleanor Fairchild, Eleanore Gregory, Barbara Heath, Ann Hutchinson, Norma Kaiser, Janice Rule, Chuck Brunner, Ted Cappy, Roscoe French, David Nillo, Harry Rogers and Swen Swenson; *From This Day On* company; *Who Done It?* Jeanne Bal as Sandra, Russell Nype as Freddie, Don Kennedy as O'Brien, Paul Reed as Rafferty, Virginia Curtis as Blodgett and Guests; *Blue Day* Martha Wright as Carol; *That's a Man Everytime* Vivienne Segal as Leslie, Marjorie Peterson as Mimsey, Jeanne Bal as Sandra and Bridesmaids; *You Appeal to Me* Vivienne Segal as Leslie and Stuart Erwin as Twigg; *Who Done It?* Virginia Curtis as Blodgett; *Let's Have a Party* Valerie Bettis as Kitty, Betty Low as Prudence, J. C. McCord as Jake and dancers Eleanor Fairchild, Eleanore Gregory, Barbara Heath, Ann Hutchinson, Norma Kaiser, Janice Rule, Chuck Brunner, Ted Cappy, Roscoe French, David Nillo, Harry Rogers and Swen Swenson; *Call It Love* Martha Wright as Carol and Mark Dawson as Vince; *Thank You, Mrs Butterfield* Wedding Guests; *Finale* company

Assistant to Tamiris, Rod Alexander; music for ballets by Ellstein, with arrangements of *Headin' for a Weddin'* and *Dreams Ago* by Genevieve Pitot

Singers: Leigh Allen, Jeanne Bal, Ruth McVayne, Joyce Mitchell, Julia Williams, Fred Bryan, Ken Carroll, Ed Gombos, John Juliano, Russell Nype and Robert Wallace

Bless You All

Broadway history: Opened Dec 14 1950   New York: Mark Hellinger Theatre   Closed Feb 24 1951 after 84 performances

Production details: production, Herman Levin and Oliver Smith; sketches, Arnold Auerbach; music and lyrics, Harold Rome; dances and staging of musical ensembles, Helen Tamiris; production design, Oliver Smith; costumes, Miles White; musical direction and vocal arrangements, Lehman Engel; lighting, Peggy Clark; staging, John C. Wilson; ballet music and arrangements, Mischa and Wesley Portnoff and Don Walker

Revue Numbers: *Bless You All* sung by Jules Munshin, Mary McCarty, Pearl Bailey, Valerie Bettis and ensemble; *Do You Know a Better Way to Make a Living?* sung by Jules Munshin and the Showgirls; *Southern Fried Chekhov* Garry Davis as Colonel Jasper Oglethorpe, Charlene Harris as Emmaline his wife, Gordon Edwards as Marmaduke his son, Mary McCarty as Marybelle his daughter and Gene Barry as The Publisher; *Don't Wanna Write about the South* sung by Mary McCarty as Marybelle, Garry Davis as the Colonel, Charlene Harris as Emmaline and Gordon Edwards as Marmaduke; *I Can Hear It Now* sung by Jane Harvey with Dorothy Etheridge as The Poor Girl, Dick Reed as The Poor Boy, Eleanor Boleyn as The Rich Girl, Donald Saddler as The Rich Boy and Carlene Carroll, Sage Fuller, Vera Lee, Ilona Murai, Emy St Just, Helen Wenzel, Swen Swenson, Joseph Gifford, Philip Nasta, Bertram Ross, John Sandal and Parker Wilson as Dancing Couples; *When* sung by Pearl Bailey with Joe Nash as A Boy and Elmira Jones-Bey as A Girl; *Back to Napoli* Robert Chisholm as Benson, Charlene Harris as Miss Kane, Garry Davis as Jaroslav, Gene Barry as Laszlo, Gwenna Lee Smith, Dell Parker, Jill Melford and Jeane Williams as The Ladies, Jules Munshin as Enrico Bonzo and Lee Barnett, Billie Kirpich, Clive Dill, Irene Riley, Betsy Holland and Ray Morrissey as The Children; *Little Things Meant So Much to Me* sung by Mary McCarty; *A Rose Is a Rose* sung by Jane Harvey and Byron Palmer with Valerie Bettis as The Rose, Joseph Gifford, Dick Reed and Bertram Ross as The Musicos, Donald Saddler as The Mobile, Joe Nash as The Sleeping Boy,

Bless You All, cont
Elmira Jones-Bey as A Piece of Sculpture and Ilona Murai, Helen Wenzel and Parker Wilson as The Revelers; *Love Letter to Manhattan* sung by Byron Palmer; *TV over the White House* with Gene Barry as Announcer, Jules Munshin as Joseph Gabriel Blow, Mary McCarty as Jane Blow, Lee Barnett as Their Son, *Love That Man* Jules Munshin as Joe with ensemble, Breakfast with Joe and Jane, *Just a Little White House* Jules Munshin as Joe, Mary McCarty as Jane and Lee Barnett as Son, *Somewhere up There* with Noel Gordon as George Washington, Garry Davis as Abe Lincoln and Robert Chisholm as Teddy Roosevelt, *Voting Blues* sung by Valerie Bettis, *Stop the Politics!* Jules Munshin as Joe and Mary McCarty as Jane, and Dell Parker as Miss Strong Constitution, Jeane Williams as Miss Natural Resources, Kris Nodland as Miss International Peace, Gwenna Lee Smith as Miss Federal Water Power and Jules Munshin as Joe and company in *Finale; Summer Dresses* sung by Byron Palmer and ensemble with Gwenna Lee Smith as The Mannequin, Jeane Williams, Blanche Grady, Sage Fuller and Emy St Just as Morning Dresses, Jill Melford, Gloria Olson, Eleanor Boleyn, Vera Lee and Billie Kirpich as Cocktail Dresses, Kris Nodland, Dell Parker, Madelyn Remini, Carlene Carroll, Ilona Murai and Helen Wenzel as Evening Dresses and Bertram Ross and Swen Swenson as Stock Boys; *The Cold War* Jules Munshin as Bill Slade and Garry Davis as The Druggist; *Take off the Coat* sung by Jane Harvey; *The Nobbiest Hobby* Jules Munshin as An Art Enthusiast, Robert Chisholm as A Clergyman, Margaret Wright as Aunty, Noel Gordon as Doctor Smith, Charlene Harris as Grandma, Grace Varik as A Nursemaid, Gene Barry as A Good Humor Man, Geraldine Hamburg as A Dowager, Gordon Edwards as An Old Fisherman, Eileen Turner as A Pretty Young Girl, Ray Morrissey as A Lifeguard, Irene Riley as A Schoolgirl and Gloria Olson, Madelyn Remini, Kris Nodland, Jill Melford, Blanche Grady, Dell Parker, Gwenna Lee Smith and Jeane Williams as Bathers; *The Desert Flame* Valerie Bettis as Desert Flame, Parker Wilson as Monsieur le Commandant, Joe Gifford, Donald McKayle, Joe Nash, Philip Nasta, Dick Reed and Bertram Ross as Gendarmes, Richard D'Arcy as Pepe Le Koko, Eleanor Boleyn, Dorothy Etheridge, Billie Kirpich, Vera Lee, Ilona Murai, Emy St Just and Helen Wenzel as Houris, Donald Saddler as The Texan, Joe Comadore and Osborne Smith as Native Drummers, John Sandal and Swen Swenson as The Torturers and Patrons, Spectators and Natives; *Peter and the P. T. A.* Mary McCarty as Mrs Weatherby, Garry Davis as Mr Fothergill, Lee Barnett as Wendy, Robert Chisholm as Captain Hook and Jane Carlyle, Betsy Holland, Dorothy Richards, Fred Bryan, Clive Dill, Kenny Smith, William Sutherland and Norval Tormsen as The Pirates; *You Never Know What Hit You—When It's Love* sung by Pearl Bailey; *The Roaring 20's Strike Back* sung by Jules Munshin and Mary McCarty; *Finale* company

Assistant to Tamiris, Daniel Nagrin

Flahooley

Broadway history: Opened May 14 1951   New York: Broadhurst Theatre   Closed June 17 1951 after 40 performances

Production details: production, Cheryl Crawford in association with Messrs Harburg and Saidy; book and direction, E. Y. Harburg and Fred Saidy; music, Sammy Fain; lyrics, E. Y. Harburg; dances and staging of musical numbers, Helen Tamiris; scenery and lighting, Howard Bay; costumes, David Ffolkes; musical direction, Maurice Levine

Musical Program: B. G. Bigelow, Inc.; A section of the Puppet Laboratory: *You Too Can Be a Puppet* Puppet Singers and *Here's to Your Illusions* sung by Barbara Cook and Jerome Courtland; Telephone Room; The Board Room; Bigelow's Toyland Bazaar: *B. G. Bigelow, Inc* sung by Executives and Personnel, dances by Sara Aman, Joe Nash, Sheldon Ossosky, Annaliese Widman, Jane Fischer and Vicki Barrett, *Najla's Song* sung by Yma Sumac and *Who Says There Ain't No Santa Claus?* sung by Jerome Courtland, Barbara Cook, Executives and Personnel; The Bigelow Hall of Fame: *Flahooley* sung and danced by Fay DeWitt, Marilyn Ross, Executives and Personnel with *Toy Band* danced by Joe Nash (Big Drum), James M. Tarbutton (Clarinet), John Anderson (Accordion), Sheldon Ossosky (Tuba), and Normand Maxon (Glockenspiel); The Puppet Laboratory: *The World Is Your Balloon* sung by Barbara Cook, Jerome Courtland and Puppet Singing Company and *He's Only Wonderful* sung by Barbara Cook and Jerome Courtland; Arabian for *"Get Happy"* sung by Yma Sumac with Irwin Corey, Nehemiah Persoff and Louis Nye; Bigelow's Inner Sanctum: *Jump, Little Chillun* danced by Sara Aman, Jane Fischer, Annaliese Widman, Normand Maxon, Joe Nash, Sheldon Ossosky and James M. Tarbutton and sung by Vicki Barrett, Carol Donn, Urylee Leonardos, Laurel Shelby, Lois Shearer, Tafi Towers, Andrew Aprea, John Anderson, Lewis Bolyard, Ray Cook, Clifford Fearl, Franklin T. Syme, Norval Tormsen and Edgar Thompson; B. G. Bigelow, Inc; City Hall Square: *Spirit of Capsulanti* sung and danced by Marilyn Ross and Townspeople and *Happy Hunting* sung by Lulu Bates, Marilyn Ross, Fay DeWitt and Townspeople; B. G. Bigelow, Inc; Bigelow's Bagdad: *Enchantment* sung by Yma Sumac and *Scheherezade* sung by Arabs and Executives; Hospital Waiting-room; Abou's Hospital Room: *Come Back, Little Genie* sung by Barbara Cook and *The Springtime Cometh* sung by Irwin Corey and danced by Elizabeth Logue; *Sing the Merry* sung by Fay DeWitt, John Anderson, Clifford Fearl, Ray Cook, Norval Tormsen, Franklin T. Syme and Lewis Bolyard; Main Street—Capsulanti: *Finale* company

Music for dances arranged by Freda Miller; puppet operators, Bil Baird, Cora Baird, Carl Harms and Franz Fazakas

Carnival in Flanders

Broadway history: Opened Sept 8 1953   New York: New Century Theatre   Closed Sept 12 1953 after 6 performances

Production details: production, Paula Stone, Mike Sloane, Johnny Burke and James Van Heusen; book, Preston Sturges; lyrics, Johnny Burke; music, James Van Heusen; direction, Preston Sturges; scenery, Oliver Smith; costumes, Lucinda Ballard; *Carnival Ballet* and staging of musical numbers, Helen Tamiris; musical direction, Harold Hastings; vocal arrangements, Elie Siegmeister; dance music for *Plundering of the Town*, Roger Adams, for *Carnival Ballet*, Elie Siegmeister and for *Spanish Dance*, Fred Herbert

Musical Numbers: *Ring the Bell* Roy Roberts as Mayor, Paul Lipson as Butcher, Bobby Vail as Barber, Paul Reed as Tailor, Lee Goodman as Innkeeper, Kevin Scott as Jan, Pat Stanley as Siska and ensemble; *The Very Necessary You* Kevin Scott as Jan and Pat Stanley as Siska; *It's a Fine Old Institution* and *I'm One of Your Admirers* Dolores Gray as Cornelia; *The Plundering of the Town* Dolores Gray as Cornelia, Matt Mattox as Courier, George Martin as 2nd Officer, with Emy St Just, John Aristides, Julie Marlowe and ensemble; *The Stronger Sex* Dolores Gray as Cornelia; *The Sudden Thrill* John Raitt as Duke; *It's an Old Spanish Custom* Dolores Gray as Cornelia and John Raitt as Duke; *A Seventeen Gun Salute* Dolores Gray as Cornelia, John Raitt as Duke, Matt Mattox as Courier, Ray Mason as 1st Officer, George Martin as 2nd Officer and ensemble; *You're Dead* Roy Roberts as Mayor, Paul Lipson as Butcher, Bobby Vail as Barber, Lee Goodman as Innkeeper and Paul Reed as Tailor; *Rainy Day* Dolores Gray as Cornelia; *Take the Word of a Gentleman* John Raitt as Duke; *The Carnival Ballet* sung by Singers of the Town and danced by Emy St Just as The Virgin, Greg O'Brien and Paul Olson as The Bats, John Aristides as The Monk, Harry Day as The Goat, Pat Stanley as The Youngest One, Jimmy Alex, Ronnie Field, Skeet Guenther, Michael Spaeth, George Martin and Richard Reed as The Plumed Swains, Sandra Devlin, Lorna Del Maestro, Pat Ferrier, Julie Marlowe, Patti Karkalits, Mary Alice Kubes and Elfrieda Zeiger as The Seven Virgins and Matt Mattox, George Martin and Jimmy Alex as The Spanish Trio; *A Moment of Your Love* Dolores Gray as Cornelia and John Raitt as Duke; *How Far Can a Lady Go?* and *It's a Fine Old Institution* Dolores Gray as Cornelia

Assistant to Tamiris, George Martin

Singers: Jean Bradley, Jean Cowles, Undine Forrest, Dolores Kempner, Mara Landi, Mary Stanton, Gloria Van Dorpe, Lee Barry, Fred Bryan, Bill Conlon, Stokley Gray, William Noble, Dick Stewart, Wesley Swails and Norman Weise

By the Beautiful Sea

Broadway history: Opened Apr 8 1954 New York: Majestic Theatre
Closed Nov 27 1954 after 270 performances

Production details: production, Robert Fryer and Lawrence Carr; book, Herbert and Dorothy Fields; music, Arthur Schwartz; lyrics, Dorothy Fields; settings and lighting, Jo Mielziner; costumes, Irene Sharaff; musical direction, Jay Blackton; production associate, Simon P. Herman; choreography, Helen Tamiris; direction, Marshall Jamison

Scenes: Backyard of Lottie Gibson's Boarding House: *The Sea Song* Shirley Booth, Boarders and Neighbors and *Mona from Arizona* John Dennio, Reid Shelton, Ray Hyson and Larry Laurence; Seaside Street in Coney Island: *Old Enough to Love* Richard France; The Midway at Coney Island: *Coney Island Boat* Shirley Booth, Robert Jennings and Visitors; The Old Mill: *Alone Too Long* Wilbur Evans; Backyard of Lottie Gibson's Boarding House: *Happy Habit* Mae Barnes; Midway at Coney Island: *Good Time Charlie* Rex Cooper, Bob Haddad, Larry Howard, Ray Kirchner, Victor Reilly, Eddie Roll and Arthur Partington dancing as Sports, Richard France, Larry Howard, Eddie Roll, Mary Harmon, Cindy Robbins and Gloria Smith as singers, and *Spicy Pictures* with Larry Laurence as The Vendor, Sigyn, Lillian Donau and Cathryn Damon as Wicked Women, Arthur Partington and Pat Ferrier as The Icemen, Gaby Monet as Serpentina Sal and *Finale* danced by Cathryn Damon, Dorothy Donau, Lillian Donau, Pat Ferrier, Sigyn, Mona Tritsch, Rex Cooper, Bob Haddad, Larry Howard, Ray Kirchner, Victor Reilly, Eddie Roll and Arthur Partington; Seaside Street in Coney Island: *Good Time Charlie* Richard France, Larry Howard, Eddie Roll, Mary Harmon, Cindy Robbins and Gloria Smith; Bedroom of Lottie Gibson's Boarding House: *I'd Rather Wake up by Myself* Shirley Booth; The Pavillion of Fun: *Hooray for George the Third* Thomas Gleason, Libi Staiger and Visitors; The Backyard of Lottie Gibson's Boarding House: *Hang Up* Mae Barnes, Boarders and Neighbors, *Alone Too Long* Shirley Booth and *More Love Than Your Love* Wilbur Evans; Stage of the Brighton Beach Theatre: *Vaudeville* Ray Kirchner, Rex Cooper and Cathryn Damon as Actors on the Bill and *Lottie Gibson Specialty* Shirley Booth; Dreamland Casino: *Throw That Anchor Away* Larry Laurence, Arthur Partington and Mary Harmon, *Dance* Gaby Monet, Arthur Partington, Richard France, Rex Cooper and Patrons and *More Love Than Your Love* Wilbur Evans; Lottie's Bedroom: *Happy Habit* Shirley Booth; Seaside Street in Coney Island: *Old Enough to Love* Richard France and Carol Leigh; Dreamland Casino: *Finale* company

Assistant to Tamiris, Daniel Nagrin; Pianist for Tamiris, Edward Johnson

Fanny

Broadway history: Opened Nov 4 1954 New York: Majestic Theatre Closed Dec 16 1956 after 888 performances

Production details: production, David Merrick and Joshua Logan; book, S. N. Behrman and Joshua Logan; music and lyrics, Harold Rome; direction, Joshua Logan; scenery and lighting, Jo Mielziner; costumes, Alvin Colt; dances, Helen Tamiris; musical direction and vocal arrangements, Lehman Engel

Musical Numbers: *Octopus Song* Gerald Price as The Admiral; *Restless Heart* William Tabbert as Marius and male ensemble; *Never Too Late for Love* Walter Slezak as Panisse and ensemble; *Cold Cream Jar Song* Walter Slezak as Panisse; *Does He Know?* Florence Henderson as Fanny and William Tabbert as Marius; *Why Be Afraid to Dance?* Ezio Pinza as Cesar, danced by Ezio Pinza as Cesar, Florence Henderson as Fanny and ensemble; *Never Too Late for Love* Ezio Pinza as Cesar, Walter Slezak as Panisse and Edna Preston as Honorine; *Shika, Shika* Nejla Ates as Arab Dancing Girl, Michael Scrittorale as An Arab Rug Seller and ensemble; *Welcome Home* Ezio Pinza as Cesar; *I Like You* Ezio Pinza as Cesar and William Tabbert as Marius; *I Have to Tell You* Florence Henderson as Fanny; *Fanny* William Tabbert as Marius; *The Sailing* Florence Henderson as Fanny, William Tabbert as Marius, Ezio Pinza as

Cesar and ensemble; *Oysters, Cockles and Mussels* ensemble; *Panisse and Son* Walter Slezak as Panisse; *Wedding Dance* danced by Charles Blackwell and ensemble; First Act *Finale* ensemble; *Birthday Song* Florence Henderson as Fanny, Edna Preston as Honorine and ensemble; *To My Wife* Walter Slezak as Panisse; *The Thought of You* William Tabbert as Marius and Florence Henderson as Fanny; *Love Is a Very Light Thing* Ezio Pinza as Cesar; *Other Hands, Other Hearts* Florence Henderson as Fanny, Ezio Pinza as Cesar and William Tabbert as Marius; *Fanny* Ezio Pinza as Cesar, Florence Henderson as Fanny and William Tabbert as Marius; *Montage* ensemble; *Be Kind to Your Parents* Florence Henderson as Fanny and Lloyd Reese as Cesario; *Cesario's Party* (Cirque Francais) Charles Blackwell, Michael de Marco, Ray Dorian, Bill Pope and Toni Wheelis as Acrobats, Wally Strauss and Steve Wiland as Pony and Trainer, Dran and Tani Seitz as Trained Seals, Betty Carr, Ronald Cecill, Norma Doggett, Michael Scrittorale, Ellen Matthews and Dolores Smith as Living Statues, Herb Banke, Mike Mason, Henry Michel and Jack Washburn as Clowns, and a Finale with Dean Crane as Aerialist and ensemble; *Welcome Home* Ezio Pinza as Cesar and Walter Slezak as Panisse

Assistant to Tamiris, Dorothy Etheridge

Additional cast not mentioned above: Tom Gleason as 1st Sailor and Garage Owner, Mohammed el Bakkar as Arab Singer, Katherine Graves as Maori Vendor, Lindsay Kirkpatrick and Margaret Baxter as Customers, Pat Finch as Oyster Fancier, Carolyn Maye and Jane House as friends of Fanny, Florence Dunlap as Fish-stall Woman, Don McHenry as Customs Inspector, Alan Carney as A Ferryboat Captain, Ruth Schumacher as a Nun and Gary Wright and Daniel Labeille as Acolytes

Fanny

Touring history: Opened Dec 25 1956   Boston: Shubert Theatre
Closed May 25 1957   Cleveland: Hanna Theatre

Production details: production, David Merrick and Joshua Logan; book, S. N. Behrman and Joshua Logan; music and lyrics, Harold Rome; direction, Joshua Logan; scenery and lighting, Jo Mielziner; costumes, Alvin Colt; dances, Helen Tamiris; musical direction and vocal arrangements, Lehman Engel

Musical Numbers: *Octopus Song* Gerald Price as Ted Beniades; *Restless Heart* Jack Washburn as Marius and male ensemble; *Never Too Late for Love* Billy Gilbert as Panisse and ensemble; *Cold Cream Jar Song* Billy Gilbert as Panisse; *Does He Know?* June Roselle as Fanny and Jack Washburn as Marius; *Why Be Afraid to Dance?* Italo Tajo as Cesar, danced by Italo Tajo as Cesar, June Roselle as Fanny and ensemble; *Never Too Late for Love* Italo Tajo as Cesar, Billy Gilbert as Panisse and Edna Preston as Honorine; *Shika, Shika* Nejla Ates as Arab Dancing Girl, Alan Carney as Escartifique and ensemble; *Welcome Home* Italo Tajo as Cesar; *I Like You* Italo Tajo as Cesar and Jack Washburn as Marius; *I Have to Tell You* June Roselle as Fanny; *Fanny* Jack Washburn as Marius; *The Sailing* June Roselle as Fanny, Jack Washburn as Marius, Italo Tajo as Cesar and ensemble; *Oysters, Cockles and Mussels* ensemble; *Panisse and Son* Billy Gilbert as Panisse; *Wedding Dance* danced by Charles Blackwell and ensemble; First Act *Finale* ensemble; *Birthday Song* June Roselle as Fanny, Edna Preston as Honorine and ensemble; *To My Wife* Billy Gilbert as Panisse; *The Thought of You* Jack Washburn as Marius and June Roselle as Fanny; *Love Is a Very Light Thing* Italo Tajo as Cesar; *Other Hands, Other Hearts,* June Roselle as Fanny, Italo Tajo as Cesar and Jack Washburn as Marius; *Fanny* Italo Tajo as Cesar, June Roselle as Fanny and Jack Washburn as Marius; *Montage* ensemble; *Be Kind to Your Parents* June Roselle as Fanny and Carson Woods as Cesario; *Cesario's Party* (Cirque Francais) Charles Blackwell, Michael de Marco, John Guarnieri and Milton Jiricka and ensemble; *Welcome Home* Italo Tajo as Cesar and Billy Gilbert as Panisse

Additional cast not mentioned above: Jim McGregor as 1st Sailor and Garage Owner, Mohammed el Bakkar as Arab Singer, Joy Lynne Sica as Lace Vendor, Ellen Matthews as Customer, Lindsay McGregor as Oyster Fancier, Ellie Zalon, Dawn Rogers, Erminie Daspit, Barbara George, Sybil Scotford, Laurie Franks, Rae MacLean and Shirlene

Fanny, touring production, cont
Gewirtz as friends of Fanny, Dulcie Cooper as Fish-stall Woman, Don McHenry as Customs Inspector, Alan Carney as A Ferryboat Captain, Marion Lauer as a Nun, John Kessler as a Priest and Berry Clifford as Acolyte. Others: Bill Keyes, Jim McAnany, Dean Crane, Douglas Foster, Al Fiorella, Ted Wills and Jim McGregor

Plain and Fancy

Broadway history: Opened Feb 24 1955   New York: Mark Hellinger Theatre   Closed Apr 14 1956 after 476 performances

Production details: production, Richard Kollmar and James W. Gardiner in association with Yvette Schumer; book, Joseph Stein and Will Glickman; lyrics, Arnold B. Horwitt; music, Albert Hague; direction, Morton Da Costa; dances and staging of musical numbers, Helen Tamiris; sets and costumes, Raoul Pene Dubois; lighting, Peggy Clark

Musical Numbers: *You Can't Miss It* Richard Derr as Dan King, Shirl Conway as Ruth Winters and ensemble; *It Wonders Me* Gloria Marlowe as Katie Yoder; *Plenty of Pennsylvania* Nancy Andrews as Emma Miller, Douglas Fletcher Rodgers as Ezra Reber, Elaine Lynn as A Young Miller and ensemble; *Young and Foolish* David Daniels as Peter Reber; *Why Not Katie?* Douglas Fletcher Rodgers as Ezra Reber and the men; *Young and Foolish* Gloria Marlowe as Katie Yoder and David Daniels as Peter Reber; *By Lantern Light* danced by Daniel Nagrin as Samuel Zook with Ann Needham, Sara Aman, Lucia Lambert, Tao Strong, Saint Amant, Crandall Diehl and Robert St Clair; *It's a Helluva Way to Run a Love Affair* Shirl Conway as Ruth Winters; *This Is All Very New to Me* sung and danced by Barbara Cook as Hilda Miller with Robert Lindgren, William Weslow and ensemble; *Plain We Live* Stefan Schnabel as Papa Yoder and ensemble; *The Shunning* company; *How Do You Raise a Barn* Stefan Schnabel as Papa Yoder, Douglas Fletcher Rodgers as Ezra Reber, Nancy Andrews as Emma Miller, Daniel Nagrin as Samuel Zook and ensemble; *Follow Your Heart* David Daniels as Peter Reber, Gloria Marlowe as Katie Yoder and Barbara Cook as Hilda Miller; *City Mouse, Country Mouse* Nancy Andrews as Emma Miller, Renee Orin as Sarah, Sybil Lamb as Esther, Muriel Shaw as Mary, Ethel May Cody as Rachel and Betty McGuire as Rebecca; *I'll Show Him!* Barbara Cook as Hilda Miller; *Carnival Ballet*: Barbara Cook as Hilda Miller, Douglas Fletcher Rodgers as Ezra Reber and company with dances *On the Midway* Daniel Nagrin as Mambo Joe, Sara Aman as Scranton Sal, Robert Lindgren as Swami, Will Able as Sailor, and Phillip Nasta, Chris Robinson and Edgar F. Thompson as Barkers and *Dance Hall* company; *Take Your Time and Take Your Pick* Barbara Cook as Katie Yoder, Richard Derr as Dan King and Shirl Conway as Ruth Winters; *Plenty of Pennsylvania* company

Assistant to Tamiris, Daniel Nagrin

Additional dancers: Imelda DeMartin, Ina Hahn, Marcia Howard, Joan Darby, Beryl Towbin, Ronnie Lee, James S. Moore and David Wood. Singers: Marilyn Bradley, Faith Daltry, Janet Hayes, Sybil Lamb, Renee Orin, Betty McGuire, Muriel Shaw, Betty Zollinger, Ray Hyson, Jack Irwin, Robert Kole, Chris Robinson, John Dennis, Herbert Surface, Edgar F. Thompson, Tim Worthington, Paul Brown and Jim Schlader

London Production of Plain and Fancy

Opened Jan 25 1956   London: Theatre Royal, Drury Lane

Production details: creation of the choreography and staging of musical numbers, Helen Tamiris, reproduced by Philip Nasta; ballet master, Harry Haythorne

Musical Numbers: *You Can't Miss It* Richard Derr as Dan King, Shirl Conway as Ruth Winters and ensemble; *It Wonders Me* Grace O'Conner as Katie Yoder; *Plenty of Pennsylvania* Virginia Somers as Emma Miller, Reed de Rouen as Ezra Reber, Hazel Mercer, Sylvia Denman, Michael Craze and Kenneth Kenner as young Millers and ensemble; *Young and Foolish* Jack Drummond as Peter Reber; *Why Not Katie?* Reed de Rouen as Ezra Reber and the men; *Young and Foolish* Grace O'Conner as Katie Yoder and Jack Drummond as Peter Reber; *By Lantern Light* danced by Harry Naughton as Samuel Zook and Audrey Farris (principal dancer) with Patricia Colburne, Leander Fedden, Mary Levack, Joan Merritt, James Dark, Paul Elsom, Brian Todd and Charles Yates; *It's a Helluva Way to Run a Love Affair* Shirl Conway as Ruth Winters; *This Is All Very New to Me* sung and danced by Joan Hovis; *Plain We Live* Malcolm Keen as Papa Yoder and ensemble; *Plain We Live* company; *How Do You Raise a Barn* company; *Follow Your Heart* Jack Drummond as Peter Reber, Grace O'Conner as Katie Yoder and Joan Hovis as Hilda Miller; *City Mouse, Country Mouse* Virginia Somers as Emma Miller with Rita Verian, Leander Fedden, Renee Fellowes, Barbara Lewis, Olive Lucius and Patricia Mortimer; *I'll Show Him!* Joan Hovis as Hilda Miller; *Carnival Ballet:* Joan Hovis as Hilda Miller, Reed de Rouen as Ezra Reber, Jack Drummond as Peter Reber and company with dances *On the Midway* Harry Naughton as Mambo Joe, Wanda Sinclair as Scranton Sal, Robert Algar as Atomic Louis, Michael Darbyshire as Sailor and Joseph Sealy and Bernard Quinn as Barkers and *Dance Hall* company; *Take Your Time and Take Your Pick* Joan Hovis as Hilda Miller, Richard Derr as Dan King and Shirl Conway as Ruth Winters; *Plenty of Pennsylvania* company

Additional cast: Ivor Emmanuel as another man and as State Trooper, Bernard Spear as Isaac Miller, Joseph Sealy as Samuel Lapp, Terence Cooper as Abner Zook, Barry Irwin as Ike Pilersheim, Frank Raynor as Moses Zook, Robert Algar as Abner Zook and Renee Fellowes as Sarah. Dancers Barbara Lewis, Olive Lucius and Patricia Mortimer also played Esther, Rebecca and Mary

Additional dancers: Patricia Berard, Sheila Cairen, Jacquiline Guise, Ann Roberts, Joy Swanson, Gilbert Brunett, Seamus Gordon, Ross Howard, Fred Owen, David Spurling and Roger Tully

Additional singers: Jenny Gaye, Dorina Gregory, June Hill, Barbara Lewis, Doreen Marlow, Jean Manning, Glen Mildren, Leonie Page, Sonia Peters, Trevor Anthony, Andrew Cole, Edwin Hill, Gilbert Harrison, Colin Kemball, Roy Lees, Mel Todd and Basil Yeo

Plain and Fancy

Touring history: United States West: Autumn 1955

Dances and musical numbers staged by Helen Tamiris; assistant to Miss Tamiris, Philip Nasta; Captain of Dancers, Jack Tygatt

Cast: Alexis Smith as Ruth Winters, Craig Stevens as Dan King, Angelo Rodriguez and Jeff Killion as men, Janet Medlin as Katie Yoder, Michael Kermoyan as Papa Yoder, Sid Marion as Isaac Miller, Libi Staiger as Emma Miller, Harry Fleer as Ezra Reber, Barbara Cook as Hilda Miller, Darryl Duran and Vicki Stern as young Millers, Richard Armbruster as Peter Reber, Lu Leonard as Rachel, Roy Fitzell as Samuel Zook, Robert Piper as Levi Stolzfuss, Jon Denton as Jacob Yoder, Jeff Killion as Samuel Lapp, Angelo Rodriguez as Abner Zook, Bob Banas as Ike Pilersheim, Robert E. Lancaster as Moses Zook, Robert Lamont as Abner Zook, Robert Driscoll as an Amishman, Joan Hovis as Bessie, Jo Ann O'Connell as Sarah, Martha Richesin as Esther, Ingeborg Kjeldsen as Rebecca, Berna Fitzell as Mary and Jerry Cardoni as State Trooper

Dancers: Roberta Ampel, Peggy Brooks, Arun Evans, Katia Geleznova, Barbara James, Gloria Kaye, Lucile C. Pickens, Barbara Ross, Carolee Winchester, Bob Banas, Jon Denton, John Grigas, Richard Gargans, David Hebel, Don Redlich, Robert Piper and Fred Zoeter

Singers: Dianne Barton, Berna Fitzell, Joan Hovis, Ingeborg Kjeldsen, Betty McNamara, Jo Ann O'Connell, Martha Richesin, Marilyn Taylor, Jerry Cardoni, Robert Cosdon, Robert Driscoll, James Hurst, Jeff Killion, Robert E. Lancaster, Robert Lamont, Angelo Rodriguez and Robert Simpson

Plain and Fancy

Touring history: United States East: Spring 1956

Dances and musical numbers staged by Helen Tamiris; assistant to Miss Tamiris, Daniel Nagrin; captain of dancers, James Moore

Cast: Evelyn Page as Ruth Winters, James Nichols as Dan King, James Schlader as a man, George Ritner as another man, Faye Winfield as Katie Yoder, Stefan Schnabel as Papa Yoder, Sammy Smith as Isaac Miller, Nancy Andrews as Emma Miller, Harry Fleer as Ezra Reber, Dran Seitz as Hilda Miller, Richard Clemence and Gloria Kayl as young Millers, David Daniels as Peter Reber, Ethel May Cody as Rachel, Daniel Nagrin as Samuel Zook, Robert Piper as Levi Stolzfuss, Will Able as Jacob Yoder, George Ritner as Samuel Lapp, Edgar Thompson as Abner Zook, James Moore as Ike Pilersheim, James Schlader as Moses Zook, Ben Parrish as Abner Zook, George Ritner as an Amishman, Betty McNamara as Bessie, Michelle Reiner or Martha Flynn as Sarah, Lee Leonard as Esther, Barbara James or Betty McGuire as Rebecca, Jeanene Anderson or Barbara James as Mary and Ray Hyson as State Trooper

Dancers: Roberta Ampel, Peggy Brooks, Arun Evans, Reby Howels, Barbara James, Gloria Kaye, Lois Rubin, Carolee Winchester, Jon Denton, John Grigas, Jack Leigh, James Moore, Don Redlich, Robert Piper, Robert St. Clair and Fred Zoeter

Singers: Jeanene Anderson, Lu Leonard, Dianne Barton, Marjorie Clozie or Martha Flynn, Barbara George, Michelle Reiner or Betty McGuire, Betty McNamara, Mary Thompson, Jimmy Allison, Robert Cosdon, Ray Hyson, Jeff Killion, Henry Lawrence, Ben Parrish, George Ritner, Jim Schlader and Edgar F. Thompson

Other publications of The New York Public Library in the field of dance:

Bournonville's London Spring. By Lillian Moore. Illustrated. 1966. 26 pages. $1.75

Dancing in Prints 1634-1870; A Portfolio of Twelve Fine Etchings, Engravings, and Color Lithographs Assembled from the Archives of the Dance Collection. With commentary by Marian Eames. 1964. 20 pages, 12 prints. Cloth portfolio. $10.00

Images of the Dance; Historical Treasures of the Dance Collection 1581-1861. By Lillian Moore. Illustrated. 1965. 86 pages. Clothbound. $6.75

New York's First Ballet Season 1792. By Lillian Moore. Second printing, 1962. 18 pages. $1.00

The Professional Appearances of Ruth St Denis & Ted Shawn; A Chronology and an Index of Dances 1906-1932. By Christena L. Schlundt. Illustrated. 1962. 85 pages. $3.00

The Professional Appearances of Ted Shawn & his Men Dancers; A Chronology and an Index of Dances 1933-1940. By Christena L. Schlundt. Illustrated. 1967. 75 pages. $3.75

Stravinsky and the Dance; A Survey of Ballet Productions 1910-1962. By Selma Jeanne Cohen. Introduction by Herbert Read. Illustrated. 1962. 60 pages. $3.00

When All the World Was Dancing: Rare and Curious Books from the Cia Fornaroli Collection. By Marian Eames. Illustrated. 18 pages. Second edition, 1958, reprinted 1971 in cooperation with Arno Press, Inc $3.00

To order, write to the Sales Office, Room 50A, The New York Public Library, Fifth Avenue & 42nd Street, New York, New York 10018. Prepayment is requested on all foreign orders and on orders totalling less than $10.00. Please make checks payable to The New York Public Library.

GV
1785
.T37
S34
1972